MASTER YOUR MONEY: A COMPREHENSIVE GUIDE TO PERSONAL FINANCE AND FRUGAL LIVING

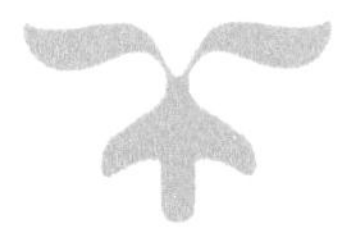

JAYANTHI R

Dedication

To my father, **Rajan M**, and my mother, **Ranjitham.**

Your unwavering love, wisdom, and sacrifices have been the guiding light of my journey.

You taught me the value of hard work, the strength in perseverance, and the beauty of dreaming big.

This book is a testament to the lessons you've instilled in me and the endless support you've given me.

With all my love and gratitude, this is for you.

Contents

CONTENTS

Foreword

In a world that often feels fast-paced and overwhelming, the pursuit of meaningful goals, financial stability, and personal growth has become more important than ever. This book is a reflection of that pursuit—a guide crafted with care, rooted in experience and aimed at empowering you to take control of your life and finances.

As the author, I began this journey with a simple yet profound mission: to share practical wisdom that could transform lives. Along the way, I discovered that success is not just about knowledge but also about having the right tools, strategies, and mindset to navigate life's challenges.

This book is not a lecture; it's a conversation. It's filled with actionable steps, relatable stories, and insights drawn from real-life experiences. Whether you are just starting your journey or looking to refine your skills, this book will meet you where you are and help you grow.

To my readers, I encourage you to approach this book with curiosity and an open mind. Take the lessons, apply them, and adapt them to your unique circumstances. Remember, growth is a process, and every step you take brings you closer to your goals.

It is my hope that this book becomes a trusted companion on your path to success and fulfilment. May it inspire you to dream bigger, achieve more, and live with purpose.

Thank you for allowing me to be a part of your journey.

With gratitude,
Jayanthi R

Preface

The idea for this book was born out of a simple yet powerful realization: the most profound transformations in life often begin with small, intentional steps. Whether it's mastering your finances, pursuing personal growth, or creating passive income streams, success is not reserved for the elite—it's achievable for anyone willing to learn, adapt, and take action.

As I embarked on this writing journey, my goal was clear: to create a resource that is practical, actionable, and inspiring. I wanted to share strategies that have worked for me and others, along with insights gained from my experiences and learnings. This book is more than a guide; it's a blueprint for taking charge of your life and creating a future filled with possibilities.

Throughout these pages, you will find a mix of proven techniques, real-world examples, and tips tailored to help you succeed in today's dynamic world. Whether you are looking to improve your financial literacy, explore innovative income opportunities, or simply gain clarity on your goals, this book is designed to meet you where you are and empower you to move forward.

Writing this book has been as much a journey of self-discovery as it has been a process of creation. It has reminded me of the power of perseverance and the value of sharing knowledge with others. My hope is that, as you read this book, you will feel inspired to take action, embrace change, and create a life that aligns with your aspirations.

Thank you for choosing to invest your time and trust in this book. I am honored to be a part of your journey, and I look forward to the incredible transformations you will achieve.

With gratitude,
Jayanthi R

Acknowledgments

This book is a result of countless moments of inspiration, hard work, and the unwavering support of those who have shaped my journey. I am deeply grateful to everyone who has contributed to making this dream a reality.

First and foremost, I want to express my heartfelt gratitude to my parents, **Rajan M** and **Ranjitham**, for their unconditional love, sacrifices, and belief in my potential. Your guidance and encouragement have been the foundation of everything I strive to achieve.

To my family and friends, thank you for cheering me on and reminding me of the importance of perseverance. Your faith in me has been a constant source of motivation.

A special thanks to my children, and my husband who have supported my thinking and contributed to my growth.

I also wish to thank my readers and supporters. Your interest, feedback, and encouragement have given me the drive to create something meaningful. This book is for you, and I hope it serves as a valuable resource in your journey.

Lastly, to everyone who has touched my life in ways big or small, whether through a kind word, a helping hand or simply by believing in my vision— thank you. This book is a testament to the collective impact of all those who have been a part of my story.

With heartfelt appreciation,
Jayanthi R

Prologue/Introduction

A New Chapter in Your Financial Journey

Money is one of the most powerful tools in our lives. It influences where we live, how we spend our time, and what opportunities we can pursue. Yet, for many, managing personal finances feels overwhelming—a source of stress and uncertainty rather than empowerment. The good news is that taking control of your finances isn't as complicated as it might seem. With the right knowledge, tools, and mindset, anyone can build a solid financial foundation and achieve their dreams.

This book, Master Your Money: A Comprehensive Guide to Personal Finance and Frugal Living, is designed to be your roadmap to financial success. Whether you're starting from scratch, looking to escape the cycle of debt, or seeking strategies to grow your wealth, this guide offers actionable advice to help you along the way.

Why Personal Finance Matters?

Personal finance isn't just about numbers—it's about freedom. When you manage your money well, you gain the freedom to make choices that align with your goals and values. Financial independence allows you to:

- Pursue a career or passion without financial worry.
- Travel, start a business, or retire early.
- Provide security and opportunities for your family.
- Manage life's challenges with resilience and confidence.

This book isn't about making you rich overnight or asking you to give up everything you enjoy. It's about helping you create a sustainable, balanced approach to money—one that allows you to live the life you want while preparing for the future.

What You'll Learn?

In this book, you'll find practical advice, real-world examples, and tools to master every aspect of your finances, including:

- **Budgeting:** Learn how to track your income and expenses and create a budget that works for you.
- **Saving:** Discover strategies to build an emergency fund, save for big goals, and plan for retirement.
- **Debt Management:** Eliminate debt with proven methods like the snowball and avalanche approaches.
- **Investing:** Understand the basics of building a diversified portfolio and growing your wealth.
    - **Frugality:** Explore cost-saving hacks and intentional spending habits that align with your lifestyle.
    - **Financial Tools:** Get recommendations on apps, systems, and templates to simplify money management.

Each chapter is packed with actionable steps that are easy to implement, no matter your current financial situation. Whether you're living paycheck to paycheck or already saving for long-term goals, there's something in this book for everyone.

Who This Book Is For?

This book is for anyone ready to take charge of their financial future. Whether you're:

- A young professional managing your first paycheck,
- A family juggling expenses and saving for the future,
- Someone drowning in debt and unsure where to start, or
- An individual ready to grow wealth and achieve financial independence...

...this guide will meet you where you are and help you move forward.

The Path to Financial Freedom

Embarking on this journey won't just improve your bank account—it will transform your mindset, habits, and life. The strategies in this book are not quick fixes; they are tools for long-term success. By committing to consistent action and embracing the principles shared here, you'll not only master your money but also build a life of greater stability, opportunity, and freedom.

So, are you ready to take control of your financial future? Let's begin your journey to financial empowerment.

Chapter 1: The Basics of Personal Finance

1.1 Understanding Net Worth

What is Net Worth?

Net worth is a snapshot of your financial health. It's the total value of everything you own (assets) minus everything you owe (liabilities).

Formula:
Net Worth = Assets - Liabilities

Assets:

- **Liquid Assets:** Easily converted to cash (e.g., cash, savings accounts).

- **Investments:** Stocks, bonds, mutual funds, retirement accounts.

- **Fixed Assets:** Real estate, vehicles, collectibles (only those with marketable value).

Liabilities:

- Debt (credit cards, loans, mortgages).

- Outstanding bills or financial obligations.

Example Calculation:

- Assets:
    - Checking account: $5,000
    - Savings account: $10,000
    - Retirement fund: $50,000
    - Car value: $15,000
    - Total Assets = $80,000
- Liabilities:
    - Credit card debt: $5,000
    - Car loan: $10,000
    - Student loan: $15,000

- ○ Total Liabilities = $30,000

Net Worth = $80,000 - $30,000 = $50,000

Why Net Worth Matters?

- It measures progress toward financial goals.

- A positive and growing net worth indicates financial health.

- A negative net worth signals the need for adjustments.

1.2 Cash Flow: The Lifeline of Your Finances

What is Cash Flow?

Cash flow is the movement of money into and out of your accounts. Positive cash flow means you earn more than you spend, while negative cash flow indicates overspending or insufficient income.

How to Calculate Cash Flow?

Cash Flow = Total Income - Total Expenses

Steps to Track Cash Flow:

1. **List All Income Sources:**

   - Salary, freelance gigs, side hustles, dividends, rental income.

   - Example: Monthly income = $4,000.

2. **List Monthly Expenses:**

   - Fixed expenses: Rent, insurance, loan payments.

   - Variable expenses: Groceries, utilities, entertainment.

3. **Track Regularly:**
   Use apps like Mint, YNAB, Chillr, Money view or spreadsheets to monitor.

1.3 Financial Literacy: The Key to Success

What is Financial Literacy?

Financial literacy is understanding and effectively using financial skills, such as budgeting, saving, and investing.

Core Areas of Financial Literacy:

1. Budgeting: Managing income and expenses.

2. Saving: Preparing for emergencies and future goals.

3. Investing: Growing wealth through compound interest.

4. Debt Management: Using credit wisely and avoiding high-interest traps.

5. Risk Management: Protecting assets with insurance and smart planning.

Why Financial Literacy is Critical?

- Avoid costly mistakes like credit card debt or under-saving for retirement.

- Make informed decisions on major purchases and investments.

- Achieve long-term goals like buying a home or starting a business.

1.4 Building the Foundation: First Steps

Step 1: Assess Your Current Situation

1. Calculate your net worth.

2. Analyse your cash flow over the past three months.

Exercise:

- Use a free online tool (like Personal Capital) or a spreadsheet to create your first net worth statement.

Step 2: Identify Your Financial Goals

1. Short-term goals (1 year): Build an emergency fund, pay off credit card debt.

2. Medium-term goals (2–5 years): Save for a vacation, down payment for a home.

3. Long-term goals (10+ years): Retirement, children's education.

   Reflection Prompt:
   Write down three financial goals for each period and why they matter to you.

Step 3: Track Your Spending

1. Spend 30 days recording every expense, from rent to a $2 coffee.

2. Use tools like Mint or a simple notebook to categorize your spending into fixed and variable expenses.

Step 4: Set a Budget

1. Once you've assessed your income, expenses, and goals, create a budget to guide your spending and saving habits. (We'll explore budgeting in detail in Chapter 2).

Step 5: Begin Building an Emergency Fund

1. Start with a goal of saving $1,000 as a basic buffer.

2. Gradually aim for 3–6 months of essential expenses.

Step 6: Educate Yourself

1. Read books like *Rich Dad Poor Dad* by Robert Kiyosaki or *The Total Money Makeover* by Dave Ramsey.

2. Follow trusted personal finance blogs or YouTube channels.

1.5 Common Pitfalls to Avoid

1. Ignoring Cash Flow:

- Failing to track income and expenses leads to financial leaks.

2. Misusing Credit Cards:

- Paying only the minimum balance or maxing out cards.

- Avoid high-interest debt by paying in full each month.

3. No Emergency Fund:

- Emergencies are inevitable. Lack of preparation can lead to debt.

4. Not Planning for the Future:

- Overlooking retirement or failing to invest early.

1.6 Tools to Get Started

Apps and Tools:

1. Budgeting: YNAB, Mint, PocketGuard, Money View, ET Money

2. Expense Tracking: EveryDollar, Goodbudget, FinArt, Chillr

3. Net Worth Tracking: Personal Capital, Groww, MyCAMS, Excel templates.

Worksheets and Templates:

- Monthly budgeting template.

- Net worth tracking sheet.

End of Chapter 1: Key Takeaways

1. Your **net worth** is a critical measure of financial health. Track it regularly.

2. Positive **cash flow** allows you to save and invest, while negative cash flow signals trouble.

3. Financial literacy is a lifelong skill—start small and build as you go.

4. The foundation of personal finance begins with understanding where you are and setting goals for where you want to go.

Chapter 2: Budgeting for Success

A well-planned budget is your roadmap to financial success. It ensures you allocate your money wisely, avoid unnecessary expenses, and move steadily toward your financial goals. In this chapter, we'll explore advanced budgeting strategies, practical examples, and tools to help you build a budget that aligns with your life goals.

2.1 Why Budgeting is Essential?

What is Budgeting?

Budgeting is the process of creating a plan for your income and expenses. It involves tracking your money, identifying spending patterns, and allocating funds to specific categories.

Why Budgeting Matters

1. **Prevents Overspending:** Keeps you aware of your limits and helps avoid debt.

2. **Reveals Financial Habits:** Identifies areas where you can cut back.

3. **Encourages Savings:** Helps you build wealth and prepare for emergencies.

4. **Promotes Financial Control:** Reduces stress by giving you clarity over your finances.

2.2 Key Principles of Effective Budgeting

1. Spend Less Than You Earn

Living within your means is the cornerstone of financial stability. Allocate funds to necessities first, then to savings and discretionary spending.

2. Align Your Budget with Your Goals

Your budget should reflect your priorities—whether it's saving for a house, paying off debt, or funding a vacation.

3. Adjust for Flexibility

Life is unpredictable. Your budget should be adaptable to account for emergencies or changing circumstances.

2.3 Steps to Build a Budget

Step 1: Calculate Your Total Income

- **Include all sources of income:** Salary, side hustles, rental income, or freelance work.
- Use after-tax income as your baseline.

Step 2: List Your Expenses

- **Fixed Expenses:** Rent, mortgage, insurance, car payments.
- **Variable Expenses:** Groceries, dining out, entertainment, transportation.
- **Irregular Expenses:** Annual subscriptions, holiday gifts, vacations.

Tip: Review your past 3 months of bank and credit card statements for an accurate view of your expenses.

Step 3: Categorize Expenses

Group your expenses into categories such as:

- Housing (rent/mortgage, utilities)
- Transportation (fuel, insurance, maintenance)
- Food (groceries, dining out)
- Health (insurance, prescriptions)
- Savings and Debt Repayment
- Entertainment and Leisure

Step 4: Set Spending Limits

Assign a limit to each category based on your income and goals. For example:

- Housing: 30% of income

  - Savings: 20%

  - Discretionary spending: 10%

2.4 Budgeting Methods

1. Zero-Based Budgeting

Assign every dollar of income to a specific purpose until your income minus expenses equals zero.
Example:

- Income: $4,000

  - Rent: $1,200
  - Utilities: $200
  - Savings: $800
  - Groceries: $600
  - Debt repayment: $500
  - Entertainment: $300
  - Miscellaneous: $400
  - Total: $4,000

Who it's for?
Detail-oriented people who want full control of their finances.

2. 50/30/20 Rule

A simplified method to allocate your income:

- **50% Needs:** Housing, food, utilities.

- **30% Wants:** Entertainment, hobbies, dining out.

- **20% Savings and Debt:** Emergency fund, investments, debt repayment.

Example:

- Income: $5,000

  - Needs: $2,500
  - Wants: $1,500
  - Savings/Debt: $1,000

Who it's for?
Beginners or those looking for an easy-to-follow structure.

3. Envelope System

Allocate physical cash or digital "envelopes" for each spending category. Once an envelope is empty, you can't spend more in that category.

Example Envelopes:

- Groceries: $500
- Entertainment: $150
- Transportation: $200

Who it's for?
Those who struggle with overspending.

4. Pay Yourself First

Prioritize saving and investing by automatically setting aside a percentage of your income before covering other expenses.

Example:

- Income: $3,000

  - Savings: $500 (set aside first)
  - Remaining: $2,500 for expenses.

Who it's for?
People focused on building savings or investment portfolios.

2.5 Common Budgeting Challenges and How to Overcome Them

Challenge 1: Irregular Income

- Solution: Base your budget on your average monthly income. Allocate surplus months to an emergency fund.

Challenge 2: Overspending on Wants

- Solution: Use a spending tracker to set daily or weekly limits for discretionary spending.

Challenge 3: Unexpected Expenses

- Solution: Maintain a buffer category in your budget or use an emergency fund for large, one-time costs.

2.6 Tools to Simplify Budgeting

Budgeting Apps:

1. **YNAB (You Need A Budget):** Zero-based budgeting tool with educational resources.

2. **Mint:** Tracks spending, bills, and categorizes expenses automatically.

3. **PocketGuard:** Helps you understand how much "extra" money you have.

4. **Walnut**: Automatically tracks expenses from SMS and categorizes them, helping users set budgets and monitor overspending.

5. **Money View**: Simplifies budgeting with automated expense tracking, budget creation, and bill reminders using SMS-based data.

6. **ET Money**: Integrates budgeting with financial planning by tracking expenses, investments, and liabilities, offering personalized insights.

7. **Cred**: Focuses on managing credit card budgets with detailed expense tracking, insights, and rewards for timely payments.

8. **FinArt**: Tracks expenses via SMS alerts for UPI, wallets, and banks, and helps users create detailed budgets with spending reports.

9. **Bishvil**: Provides manual budgeting tools with customizable income and expense categories, generating monthly and yearly reports.

10. **Kuvera**: Combines budgeting with investment tracking and financial goal setting for a holistic financial overview.

11. **Chillr**: Tracks UPI and bank transactions, monitors account balances, and simplifies budgeting for users managing multiple accounts.

12. **Monefy**: Offers manual expense and budget tracking with easy-to-read charts and customizable spending categories.

13. **HomeBudget with Sync**: Family-oriented budgeting tool that tracks shared income, expenses, and recurring bills across multiple devices.

Spreadsheets:

Use templates from Google Sheets or Excel to create custom budgets.

2.7 Staying Motivated: Tips to Stick to Your Budget

1. Celebrate Small Wins

Each month you stick to your budget, and reward yourself in a modest, budget-friendly way.

2. Automate Where Possible

Set up automatic transfers to savings and bill payments to reduce effort and temptation.

3. Involve Your Family

If you share finances with a partner or family, involve them in budgeting to ensure everyone is on the same page.

End of Chapter 2: Key Takeaways

1. Budgeting is essential for aligning your spending with your goals.

2. Choose a method that works best for your personality and lifestyle (e.g., zero-based, 50/30/20).

3. Track your progress monthly and adjust as needed.

Chapter 3: Building a Savings Strategy

Saving is the cornerstone of personal finance. A solid savings strategy ensures financial security, helps you achieve your goals, and protects you during unexpected events. In this chapter, we'll dive deep into the purpose of saving, how to save effectively, and strategies to accelerate your savings journey.

3.1 Why Saving Matters?

The Importance of Savings

1. **Financial Security:** An emergency fund prevents you from falling into debt during unexpected events like job loss, medical expenses, or car repairs.

2. **Goal Achievement:** Savings help you fund life goals such as buying a house, travelling, starting a business, or retiring comfortably.

3. **Stress Reduction:** Knowing you have money set aside reduces financial anxiety.

3.2 Types of Savings to Prioritize

1. Emergency Fund

An emergency fund acts as a financial cushion for unexpected expenses.

- **Recommended Amount:** 3–6 months of essential living expenses (rent, utilities, groceries, insurance).

- **Where to Keep It:** High-yield savings accounts or money market accounts for easy access and slight growth.

- **Building Your Fund:** Start with a small target, like $1,000, and gradually increase it.

2. Short-Term Savings

These are for goals within the next 1–3 years, such as:

- Vacations

- Weddings

- A new car

Where to Save:

- Savings accounts

- Certificates of deposit (CDs) for slightly higher interest if you don't need immediate access.

3. Long-Term Savings

For goals more than 3 years away, like:

- Buying a home

- Starting a business

- Funding your child's education

Where to Save?

- Low-risk investments like bonds or diversified mutual funds.

3.3 Building an Effective Savings Plan

Step 1: Define Your Savings Goals

Identify what you're saving for and categorize each goal as short-term or long-term.

Examples:

- Short-term: $3,000 for a vacation in 12 months.

- Long-term: $50,000 for a home down payment in 5 years.

Step 2: Calculate How Much You Need

Break your savings goals into smaller, actionable targets.

Example Calculation:

- Goal: Save $3,000 for a vacation in 12 months.

- Monthly Savings = $3,000 \div 12 = $250 per month.

Step 3: Automate Your Savings

1. **Direct Deposit:** Set up automatic transfers from your paycheck to your savings account.

2. **Bank Tools:** Use apps that round up your purchases and save the change (e.g., Acorns).

Step 4: Prioritize High-Impact Savings

Focus on building an emergency fund first, then allocate savings toward other goals based on priority and urgency.

3.4 Strategies to Boost Savings

1. Create a "Pay Yourself First" System

Treat savings as a non-negotiable expense. Allocate a percentage of your income (e.g., 20%) to savings before spending on anything else.

Example:

- Monthly Income: $4,000
- Savings Allocation: $800 (20%)
- Remaining for expenses: $3,200

2. Try Savings Challenges

Gamify your savings efforts to stay motivated.

Popular Challenges:

- **52-Week Challenge:** Save $1 in week 1, $2 in week 2, and so on. By week 52, you'll have $1,378.

- **No-Spend Month:** Commit to avoid non-essential spending for 30 days and divert the savings to your goals.

3. Cut Back on Non-Essential Expenses

Small adjustments can lead to significant savings over time.

- **Dining Out:** Limit restaurant visits and cook more at home.

- **Subscriptions:** Cancel unused or unnecessary subscriptions.

- **Impulse Purchases:** Wait 24 hours before making non-essential purchases.

Example:

- Skipping a $5 coffee 5 times a week = $25/week = $1,300/year.

4. Use Windfalls Wisely

Unexpected income, like tax refunds or bonuses, can be a savings accelerator. Allocate at least 50–75% of any windfall toward your savings goals.

3.5 Common Saving Mistakes to Avoid

1. Not Starting Early

The longer you delay, the harder it becomes to reach your financial goals due to lost opportunities for compound interest.

2. Keeping All Savings in a Low-Interest Account

While savings accounts are safe, their low returns may not outpace inflation. Diversify with high-yield accounts, CDs, or investments for long-term savings.

3. Dipping into Savings for Non-Essentials

Maintain discipline by separating emergency funds from other savings and using them only for legitimate needs.

3.6 Tools and Resources for Savers

Savings Apps:

1. **Digit:** Analyses your spending and saves small amounts automatically.

2. **Qapital:** Lets you set savings goals and rules (e.g., save $5 every time you skip dining out).

3. **Chime:** Offers automatic savings features, such as rounding up purchases to save the difference.

4. **Jar**: Micro-savings app that rounds up daily expenses and invests spare change in digital gold.

3.7 Saving for Retirement

Saving for retirement is critical and requires long-term planning. We'll explore this topic further in **Chapter 6**, but here's an overview:

- Start early to take advantage of compound interest.

- Contribute consistently to retirement accounts like a 401(k) or IRA (In India, retirement accounts like EPF or PPF or NPS).

- Increase contributions when your income rises.

End of Chapter 3: Key Takeaways

1. Prioritize building an emergency fund to cover 3–6 months of essential expenses.

2. Set clear savings goals and automate the process to stay consistent.

3. Use tools and strategies like savings challenges and cutting non-essential expenses to accelerate progress.

4. Avoid common mistakes, like starting too late or keeping savings stagnant in low-interest accounts.

Chapter 4: Debt Management in Detail

Managing debt is a critical aspect of personal finance. While debt can be useful for achieving goals like buying a home or financing education, excessive or poorly managed debt can jeopardize your financial stability. In this chapter, we'll explore how to understand, manage, and eliminate debt effectively.

4.1 Understanding Debt

What is Debt?

Debt is money borrowed from a lender with the agreement to repay it over time, often with interest. It is a financial obligation that can take many forms.

Types of Debt

1. **Secured Debt:** Backed by collateral (e.g., a house or car).

   o   Examples: Mortgage, auto loan.

   o   Risk: Defaulting could result in losing the asset.

2. **Unsecured Debt:** No collateral; based on your creditworthiness.

   o   Examples: Credit cards, personal loans, medical bills.

   o   Risk: Higher interest rates due to greater risk for the lender.

3. **Revolving Debt:** Borrowing up to a credit limit and repaying repeatedly.

   o   Example: Credit cards.

4. **Instalment Debt:** Fixed payments over a set period.

   o   Examples: Student loans, auto loans.

5. **Good Debt vs. Bad Debt:**

   o   **Good Debt:** Helps build wealth (e.g., a mortgage or student loan).

o **Bad Debt:** Used for depreciating assets or non-essential purchases (e.g., credit card debt for luxuries).

4.2 Assessing Your Debt Situation

Step 1: Calculate Your Total Debt

Make a list of all debts, including:

- Creditor name

- Outstanding balance

- Interest rate

- Minimum monthly payment

- Payment due date

Step 2: Calculate Your Debt-to-Income Ratio (DTI)

Formula:
DTI = (Total Monthly Debt Payments ÷ Monthly Gross Income) × 100

Example:

- Monthly Debt Payments: $1,000
- Monthly Income: $4,000
- DTI = ($1,000 ÷ $4,000) × 100 = 25%

What DTI Indicates:

- Below 36%: Healthy debt level.

- 37–49%: Manageable but needs attention.

- 50% or more: Risky financial situation.

4.3 Strategies for Managing Debt

1. Create a Debt Repayment Plan

A structured repayment plan ensures you tackle debt systematically.

Debt Repayment Methods:

a. Debt Snowball Method:

- Focus on paying off the smallest debt first while making minimum payments on others.

- Motivation grows as you eliminate smaller balances.

Example:

1. Debt A: $500 at 5% interest.

2. Debt B: $2,000 at 10% interest.

3. Debt C: $5,000 at 15% interest.

Pay off Debt A first, then move to Debt B, and so on.

b. Debt Avalanche Method:

- Prioritize paying off the debt with the highest interest rate first to save on interest.

Example:

1. Debt A: $5,000 at 15% interest.

2. Debt B: $2,000 at 10% interest.

3. Debt C: $500 at 5% interest.

Focus on Debt A first, then Debt B, and finally Debt C.

Which to Choose?

- Snowball: Best for emotional wins and motivation.

- Avalanche: Best for saving money on interest.

2. Consolidate Debt

Combine multiple debts into one with a lower interest rate or a single payment.

Options:

- **Personal Loan:** Use a loan with a lower interest rate to pay off high-interest debts.

- **Balance Transfer Credit Card:** Transfer high-interest credit card balances to a card with 0% introductory APR.

Caution:
Avoid accumulating new debt after consolidation.

3. Negotiate with Creditors

If you're struggling to make payments, reach out to creditors to request:

- Lower interest rates.

- Waived late fees.

- A temporary payment plan.

4. Avoid Adding New Debt

- Freeze credit card usage until debts are under control.

- Delay major purchases unless necessary.

- Focus on paying cash for smaller expenses.

4.4 Managing Credit Card Debt

Credit Card Do's and Don'ts

- **Do:** Pay your balance in full each month to avoid interest charges.

- **Don't:** Only pay the minimum due; this leads to higher interest costs.

How to Lower Credit Card Interest?

1. Transfer balances to a 0% APR card.

2. Request a lower interest rate from your provider.

3. Pay more than the minimum payment to reduce the principal faster.

4.5 Tackling Student Loan Debt

Federal Loans vs. Private Loans

- **Federal Loans:** Offer income-driven repayment plans, deferment, and forgiveness programs.

- **Private Loans:** Typically have less flexibility but may offer refinancing options.

Strategies to Pay Off Student Loans:

1. **Enroll in Income-Driven Repayment Plans:** Payments are based on your income, and balances may be forgiven after a set number of years.

2. **Refinance for Lower Interest Rates:** If you have strong credit and stable income, refinancing can reduce costs.

3. **Make Extra Payments:** Apply extra money directly to the loan principal.

4.6 Preventing Debt in the Future

1. Create an Emergency Fund

An emergency fund prevents you from relying on credit cards during financial emergencies.

2. Budget Carefully

Include a "debt repayment" category in your monthly budget until all debts are cleared.

3. Limit Credit Card Usage

Use credit cards only for planned purchases and pay off the balance in full every month.

4. Avoid Lifestyle Inflation

As your income increases, maintain your current lifestyle and use extra money to pay off debt or save.

4.7 Tools for Debt Management

Apps and Tools:

1. **Debt Payoff Planner:** Helps you track progress and choose repayment strategies.

2. **Tally:** Automatically manages credit card payments to minimize interest.

3. **Mint:** Tracks your overall financial picture, including debts.

4.8 Emotional and Psychological Aspects of Debt

1. Addressing Debt-Related Stress

- Talk to a financial counsellor for guidance.

- Break your debt into manageable milestones to reduce overwhelm.

2. Building a Positive Mindset

- View debt repayment as an investment in your future.

- Celebrate small wins, like paying off one debt entirely.

4.9 Improving Your Credit Score

Why Your Credit Score Matters?

A good credit score helps to secure loans at lower interest rates, saving money over time.

How Credit Scores Are Calculated?

1. **Payment History (35%):** Timely payments boost your score.

2. **Credit Utilization (30%):** Keep usage below 30% of available credit.

3. **Credit History Length (15%):** Longer histories improve your score.

4. **Credit Mix (10%):** A variety of credit types is favourable.

5. **New Credit (10%):** Too many recent applications can hurt your score.

Tips to Improve Your Credit Score

1. Pay bills on time, every time.

2. Reduce high credit card balances.

3. Avoid closing old accounts to preserve credit history.

4. Limit new credit applications.

5. Regularly check your credit report for errors.

End of Chapter 4: Key Takeaways

1. Understand your debt by calculating your total balance and debt-to-income ratio.

2. Choose a repayment method (Snowball or Avalanche) and commit to it.

3. Avoid accumulating new debt by budgeting, cutting expenses, and creating an emergency fund.

4. Use tools like apps or professional advice to manage and track your debt progress.

5. Improve your credit score to lower borrowing costs.

Chapter 5: Investing for Wealth Creation

Investing is one of the most powerful ways to grow your wealth, achieve financial freedom, and build a secure future. While saving is essential, investing enables you to put your money to work, leveraging the power of compound interest and market growth to build wealth over time. In this chapter, we'll cover the fundamentals of investing, different asset classes, strategies for beginners and experienced investors, and the tools you need to get started.

5.1 Why Invest?

1. Build Wealth Over Time

Investing allows your money to grow through the power of compounding. This means your investments earn returns, and those returns generate additional earnings over time.

Example of Compound Interest:

- Investment: $10,000
- Annual Return: 7%
- After 10 Years: $19,671
- After 20 Years: $38,697

2. Beat Inflation

Inflation reduces the purchasing power of money over time. Investing in assets that grow faster than inflation (e.g., stocks, real estate) ensures your wealth retains its value.

3. Achieve Financial Goals

Whether it's buying a home, funding education, or retiring comfortably, investing helps you grow the wealth needed to achieve these long-term goals.

5.2 Understanding Risk and Return

The Risk-Return Trade-off

The higher the potential return on an investment, the greater the risk involved.

- **Low Risk, Low Return:** Savings accounts, government bonds.

- **High Risk, High Return:** Stocks, cryptocurrencies.

Key Principle: Diversify your portfolio to balance risk and reward.

Risk Tolerance

Your risk tolerance depends on your financial goals, investment timeline, and comfort with market volatility.

- **Aggressive Investors:** Younger investors with long timelines can afford to take higher risks.

- **Conservative Investors:** Near-retirement individuals may prefer safer investments.

5.3 Types of Investment Assets

1. Stocks

What Are Stocks?
Stocks represent ownership in a company. When you buy a stock, you own a small part of that business.

Benefits:

- High potential for growth.

- Opportunity to earn dividends.

Risks:

- Market volatility can lead to losses in the short term.

2. Bonds

What Are Bonds?
Bonds are loans you give to a government or corporation in exchange for regular interest payments and the return of the principal amount at maturity.

Benefits:

- Stable income.

- Lower risk compared to stocks.

Risks:

- Lower returns.

- Inflation can erode purchasing power.

3. Mutual Funds

What Are Mutual Funds?
A mutual fund pools money from multiple investors to invest in a diversified portfolio of stocks, bonds, or other assets.

Benefits:

- Professional management.

- Diversification with a single investment.

Risks:

- Fees can eat into returns.

- Performance depends on the fund manager.

4. Exchange-Traded Funds (ETFs)

What Are ETFs?

ETFs are like mutual funds but trade on stock exchanges like individual stocks.

Benefits:

- Low fees.

- Easy to trade.

Risks:

- Market volatility affects value.

5. Real Estate

What Is Real Estate Investing?
Investing in property to earn rental income or sell for a profit.

Benefits:

- Tangible asset.

- Potential for regular income.

Risks:

- Illiquid and requires significant capital.

- Market downturns can affect value.

6. Cryptocurrencies

What Are Cryptocurrencies?
Digital currencies like Bitcoin and Ethereum use blockchain technology.

Benefits:

- High growth potential.

- Decentralized and accessible.

Risks:

- Extreme volatility.

- Regulatory uncertainty.

5.4 Getting Started with Investing

Step 1: Set Your Goals

Define what you're investing for:

- Short-term goals: Less than 5 years (e.g., vacation, car purchase).

- Long-term goals: More than 5 years (e.g., retirement, buying a house).

Step 2: Build an Emergency Fund

Before investing, ensure you have 3–6 months' worth of expenses saved in an emergency fund.

Step 3: Learn the Basics

Educate yourself about key investing concepts such as:

- Asset allocation.

- Diversification.

- Risk management.

Step 4: Open an Investment Account

Types of accounts to consider:

1. **Brokerage/Demat Accounts:** For buying and selling stocks, bonds, ETFs, etc.

2. **Retirement Accounts (e.g., IRA, 401(k), EPF, PPF):** Tax-advantaged accounts designed for retirement savings.

Popular Brokerage Platforms:

- Robinhood (user-friendly for beginners).

- Fidelity (broad range of investment options).

- Vanguard (low-cost index funds).

- Zerodha (user-friendly for beginners and advanced traders with low-cost brokerage).

- Upstox (cost-effective platform with modern, intuitive tools).

- Angel One (full-service features with discounted flat-rate brokerage).

- Groww (beginner-friendly app focused on simplicity and mutual fund investments).

- ICICI Direct (reliable full-service broker with a 3-in-1 account integration).

- HDFC Securities (secure platform for HDFC Bank account holders with advisory services).

- Motilal Oswal (research-driven platform with advanced portfolio management services).

- 5paisa (affordable flat-rate brokerage with robot-advisory for mutual funds).

- Sharekhan (trusted platform for research-focused investors and advanced traders).

- Paytm Money (low-cost app designed for beginners and mobile-first users).

Step 5: Start Small

Begin with a small amount to get comfortable with the process. You can invest in:

- Fractional shares of stocks.

- Low-cost index funds or ETFs.

5.5 Investment Strategies

1. Passive Investing

Invest in index funds or ETFs that track market performance.

- **Benefits:** Low fees, requires little effort.

- **Example:** S&P 500 Index Fund.

2. Active Investing

Actively buy and sell stocks or other assets to outperform the market.

- **Benefits:** Potential for higher returns.

- **Risks:** Higher fees and time commitment.

3. Dollar-Cost Averaging (DCA)

Invest a fixed amount at regular intervals, regardless of market conditions.

- **Benefits:** Reduces the impact of market volatility.

- **Example:** Invest $500 monthly into an ETF.

4. Growth vs. Value Investing

- **Growth Investing:** Focus on companies with high potential for future growth (e.g., tech startups).

- **Value Investing:** Invest in undervalued companies trading below their intrinsic value.

5. Diversification

Spread your investments across different asset classes (stocks, bonds, real estate) and sectors to reduce risk.

5.6 Monitoring and Adjusting Your Portfolio

1. Track Performance

Regularly review your portfolio to ensure it aligns with your goals.

2. Rebalance Periodically

Adjust your portfolio to maintain your desired asset allocation.

Example:

- Goal: 60% stocks, 40% bonds.

- If stocks grow to 70%, sell some stocks and buy bonds to rebalance.

3. Stay Informed

Keep up with market trends and economic news but avoid overreacting to short-term fluctuations.

5.7 Avoiding Common Investment Mistakes

1. **Starting Late:** The earlier you start, the more time your investments must grow.

2. **Emotional Investing:** Avoid making decisions based on fear or greed.

3. **Neglecting Diversification:** Concentrating investments in one asset class increases risk.

4. **Ignoring Fees:** High fees can significantly reduce your returns over time.

End of Chapter 5: Key Takeaways

1. Investing is essential for building wealth and achieving financial goals.

2. Understand the risk-return trade-off and choose investments that align with your risk tolerance.

3. Start with basic assets like ETFs or mutual funds and diversify your portfolio.

Regularly monitor and adjust your investments to stay on track.

Chapter 6: Retirement Planning

Retirement planning is one of the most critical components of personal finance. It ensures you can maintain your lifestyle and financial independence when you are no longer working. In this chapter, we'll cover the essentials of retirement planning, from understanding the basics of retirement savings accounts to crafting a retirement strategy tailored to your goals.

6.1 Understanding Retirement Planning

What Is Retirement Planning?

Retirement planning involves setting financial goals and taking steps to accumulate sufficient savings and investments to support yourself during retirement. This includes:

1. Estimating how much money you will need in retirement.

2. Identifying sources of income (e.g., pensions, investments).

3. Creating a saving and investing strategy to reach your goals.

Why Retirement Planning Is Essential?

1. **Longer Life Expectancy:** Advances in healthcare mean people are living longer, requiring more savings to cover additional years of expenses.

2. **Rising Costs:** Inflation increases the cost of living over time, meaning your money must stretch further in retirement.

3. **Financial Independence:** Proper planning ensures you won't need to rely on family or government assistance.

4. **Peace of Mind:** Knowing you're financially prepared reduces stress and allows you to enjoy your retirement.

6.2 Estimating Your Retirement Needs

Step 1: Define Your Retirement Lifestyle

Think about the kind of lifestyle you want:

- Will you travel frequently?

- Do you plan to downsize your home?

- Will you pursue hobbies that require significant funding?

Tip: Be realistic about future expenses, considering both needs (housing, healthcare) and wants (leisure, travel).

Step 2: Calculate Your Annual Retirement Expenses

- **Essential Expenses:** Housing, food, healthcare, utilities, insurance, and taxes.

- **Discretionary Expenses:** Entertainment, travel, hobbies.

Rule of Thumb: Aim to replace 70–80% of your pre-retirement income to maintain your current lifestyle.

Step 3: Factor in Inflation

Inflation erodes the purchasing power of money over time. Assume an average inflation rate of 2–3% annually when estimating future expenses.

Example:
If you need $50,000 per year today, in 20 years (at 3% inflation), you will need about $90,305 annually.

Step 4: Consider Healthcare Costs

Healthcare is often one of the largest expenses in retirement. Plan for:

- Medicare or private insurance premiums.

- Out-of-pocket expenses (medications, treatments, long-term care).

Step 5: Account for Longevity

To avoid outliving your savings, plan for a retirement lasting 20–30 years or more, depending on your health and family history.

6.3 Retirement Savings Accounts

1. Defined Contribution Plans

These are employer-sponsored plans where both you and your employer can contribute.

Examples:

- **401(k) (US):** Tax-advantaged plan where contributions reduce taxable income.

- **NPS (India):** National Pension System allowing flexible contributions.

Benefits:

- Tax advantages (pre-tax or tax-deferred growth).

- Potential employer match.

2. Individual Retirement Accounts (IRAs)

- **Traditional IRA:** Contributions may be tax-deductible, but withdrawals are taxed.

- **Roth IRA:** Contributions are made after tax, but withdrawals are tax-free.

Here are the retirement-focused accounts in India:

- **Employees' Provident Fund (EPF):** Employer and employee contribute a fixed percentage of salary; withdrawals are tax-free after a specific period.

- **Public Provident Fund (PPF):** Contributions are tax-deductible, and both interests earned, and withdrawals are tax-free.

- **National Pension System (NPS):** Contributions are tax-deductible, with partial taxability on withdrawals; a portion is mandatorily annuitized.

- **Senior Citizens Savings Scheme (SCSS):** Tax-deductible contributions with regular interest payouts; interest earned is taxable.

- **Atal Pension Yojana (APY):** Fixed pension post-retirement based on contributions; government co-contribution for eligible users.

- **Voluntary Provident Fund (VPF):** Optional extension of EPF with tax-deductible contributions; interest and withdrawals are tax-free.

3. Pensions

A defined benefit plan where employers promise a fixed monthly payment in retirement. These are becoming less common but are still a reliable source of income for those eligible.

4. Personal Savings and Investments

- **Taxable Investment Accounts:** Flexible but subject to capital gains taxes.

- **Real Estate:** Rental properties or downsizing your home can provide income.

5. Government Programs

Programs like Social Security (US) or the Employees' Provident Fund (India) provide a safety net but may not be sufficient to cover all retirement expenses.

6.4 How to Save for Retirement?

1. Start Early

The earlier you begin saving, the more time your money must grow through compounding.

Example:

- Starting at Age 25: Save $300/month at 7% annual return. By 65, you'll have $726,000.

- Starting at Age 35: Save $600/month at 7% annual return. By 65, you'll have $648,000.

2. Contribute Consistently

Make regular contributions to retirement accounts, even during economic downturns.

3. Maximize Employer Contributions

If your employer offers a matching contribution, take full advantage. It's essentially free money.

6.5 Investing for Retirement

Asset Allocation by Age

Your investment mix should reflect your time horizon and risk tolerance.

- **In Your 20s and 30s:** Focus on growth assets like stocks.

- **In Your 40s and 50s:** Gradually increase exposure to bonds and stable assets.

- **In Your 60s and Beyond:** Prioritize capital preservation with more conservative investments.

Target-Date Funds

These funds automatically adjust your asset allocation as you approach retirement, making them ideal for hands-off investors.

India doesn't have direct equivalents to **Target-Date Funds** (TDFs) commonly found in the U.S., but there are some investment options with similar concepts that automatically adjust or are designed for long-term goals. These are structured to help investors save for retirement with risk levels that may change over time. Here are some Indian alternatives:

- **Life Stage Funds by NPS (National Pension System)**: Automatically adjusts asset allocation (equity, corporate bonds, government bonds) based on the investor's age, reducing risk as retirement approaches.

- **Retirement Mutual Funds**: Designed specifically for retirement savings, these funds gradually reduce equity exposure as the retirement date nears. Examples include **HDFC Retirement Savings Fund** and **Tata Retirement Savings Fund**.

- **Insurance-Based Retirement Plans**: ULIP-based retirement plans offered by insurers like LIC or ICICI Prudential, which shift asset allocation towards safer investments as you near retirement age.

6.6 Creating a Retirement Plan

Step 1: Set a Target Retirement Age

Determine when you want to retire and how many years you'll need to fund.

Step 2: Estimate Income Sources

Identify all potential income streams:

- Pensions.

- Social Security.

- Dividends, rental income, or annuities.

Step 3: Plan for Withdrawals

Adopt a sustainable withdrawal strategy to avoid depleting your savings prematurely.

Rule of Thumb: The **4% Rule** suggests withdrawing 4% of your savings annually in retirement.

6.7 Avoiding Common Retirement Planning Mistakes

1. **Starting Too Late:** Procrastination reduces the power of compounding.

2. **Underestimating Expenses:** Ensure you account for inflation and unexpected costs.

3. **Relying Solely on Government Benefits:** Social Security or pensions are not guaranteed to cover all expenses.

4. **Failing to Diversify:** Concentrating assets in one area increases risk.

6.8 Managing Retirement During Retirement

1. **Create a Budget**

   Monitor your spending to ensure your savings last.

2. **Rebalance Your Portfolio**

Continue to adjust your asset allocation to reduce risk.

3. **Plan for Healthcare and Long-Term Care**

Consider insurance policies like long-term care insurance to protect against high medical costs.

End of Chapter 6: Key Takeaways

1. Start retirement planning early to take advantage of compounding.

2. Calculate your retirement needs based on lifestyle, longevity, and healthcare costs.

3. Utilize tax-advantaged accounts like 401(k)s, IRAs, EPF, PPF and pensions.

4. Diversify your investments and adjust your strategy as you age.

Avoid common mistakes like starting late or underestimating expenses.

Chapter 7: Building Passive Income Streams

Passive income is money earned with minimal effort on an ongoing basis. It is a key strategy for achieving financial freedom, as it allows you to generate income even while you sleep, travel, or focus on other pursuits. In this chapter, we'll explore the concept of passive income, its benefits, popular sources, and actionable steps to create sustainable passive income streams.

7.1 Understanding Passive Income

What Is Passive Income?

Passive income is revenue earned without direct involvement in day-to-day operations. Unlike active income, which requires your time and effort (like a job), passive income builds on initial work or investment to generate ongoing returns.

Why Is Passive Income Important?

1. **Financial Independence:** It reduces reliance on active income and helps cover living expenses.

2. **Time Freedom:** Allows you to focus on personal passions or other goals.

3. **Wealth Accumulation:** Creates additional revenue streams, which can be reinvested to build wealth.

4. **Emergency Buffer:** Provides a safety net during periods of unemployment or reduced income.

Myths About Passive Income

1. **"It's Completely Hands-Off":** Most passive income streams require initial effort or ongoing maintenance.

2. **"It's Quick Money":** Building sustainable passive income takes time and strategy.

7.2 Types of Passive Income Streams

1. Investments

a. Dividend Stocks

- **What Are They?** Stocks from companies that pay regular dividends to shareholders.
- **Benefits:** Steady income with potential for capital appreciation.
- **Examples:** Utilities, large-cap companies like Coca-Cola or Procter & Gamble.

b. Real Estate

- **Rental Properties:** Buy property to earn rental income.
- **REITs (Real Estate Investment Trusts):** Invest in real estate portfolios without direct ownership.
- **Benefits:** Long-term appreciation and regular income.
- **Risks:** Market fluctuations and maintenance costs.

c. Bonds

- **What Are They?** Fixed-income securities issued by governments or corporations.
- **Benefits:** Stable, predictable income with lower risk.

2. Digital Products and Online Ventures

a. E-Books

- **What Are They?** Write a book and sell it on platforms like Amazon Kindle Direct Publishing (KDP).
- **Effort:** Initial time investment in writing, editing, and marketing.

b. Online Courses

- **What Are They?** Create and sell courses on platforms like Udemy or Teachable.
- **Benefits:** High demand for skills-based learning.

c. Affiliate Marketing

- **What Is It?** Earn commissions by promoting products or services.

- **Platforms:** Amazon Associates, ClickBank.

d. Ad Revenue from Content

- **YouTube:** Monetize videos through ads.

- **Blogs:** Use ad networks like Google AdSense.

3. Licensing

a. Royalties

- **What Are They?** Earn from intellectual property like music, patents, or art.

- **Example:** A songwriter earns royalties every time their song is played.

b. Software Development

- Develop apps, plugins, or software and sell licenses or subscriptions.

4. Side Business Ventures

a. Dropshipping

- Operate an e-commerce store without managing inventory.

- Platforms: Shopify, WooCommerce.

b. Peer-to-Peer Lending

- Lend money through platforms like Prosper, LendingClub, Faircent or LenDenClub to earn interest.

5. Other Notable Sources

- **Cash-Back Rewards:** Credit cards and apps that offer rewards on purchases.

- **Automated Businesses:** Franchises or automated kiosks.

7.3 How to Build Passive Income Streams?

Step 1: Assess Your Strengths and Resources

- **Time:** Do you have time to create content or manage real estate?
- **Money:** Do you have capital to invest in stocks, bonds, or property?
- **Skills:** Can you write, teach, or develop digital products?

Step 2: Start with One Stream

Focus on one income source before diversifying. This ensures you allocate sufficient time and effort to make it successful.

Step 3: Automate Where Possible

- Use scheduling tools for content creation.
- Employ property managers for real estate.
- Use dividend reinvestment plans (DRIPs) for stock dividends.

Step 4: Reinvest Profits

Use earnings from passive income streams to:

- Grow your existing ventures.
- Diversify into new income sources.

7.4 Overcoming Challenges

1. Time Investment

Solution: Break projects into smaller, manageable tasks and set deadlines.

2. Initial Costs

Solution: Start with low-cost options like writing an e-book or affiliate marketing.

3. Maintenance

Solution: Allocate a few hours monthly to monitor and maintain income streams.

7.5 Passive Income Strategies for Beginners

1. Start Small with Savings

- Open a high-yield savings account.

- Invest in low-cost ETFs or index funds.

2. Leverage Technology

- Create and market digital products using platforms like Canva, Skillshare, or Shopify.

3. Collaborate

Partner with experts to reduce the burden of creating and managing income streams.

7.6 Passive Income for Financial Freedom

To achieve financial independence:

1. Calculate your financial independence number (e.g., annual expenses x 25).

2. Focus on building diversified income streams to cover your expenses.

3. Continuously reinvest surplus income to compound your wealth.

End of Chapter 7: Key Takeaways

1. Passive income requires initial effort or investment but creates lasting financial benefits.

2. Popular sources include dividend stocks, real estate, online courses, and royalties.

3. Start small, automate, and reinvest to grow your income streams.

Diversify across multiple sources to mitigate risks.

Chapter 8: Emergency Fund Essentials

An emergency fund is a cornerstone of financial stability and resilience. Life is full of uncertainties, and an emergency fund ensures that you can manage unexpected expenses without derailing your financial goals. Whether it's a medical emergency, car repair, or job loss, having money set aside provides peace of mind and prevents reliance on high-interest debt.

In this chapter, we will explore what an emergency fund is, why it's crucial, how to build one, and how to manage it effectively.

8.1 What Is an Emergency Fund?

An emergency fund is a reserve of money set aside specifically to cover unexpected financial emergencies.

- It's not for planned expenses like vacations or luxury purchases.

- It acts as a financial cushion to protect you from falling into debt during challenging times.

Characteristics of a Good Emergency Fund

1. **Easily Accessible:** Should be liquid and readily available in a savings or money market account.

2. **Dedicated Purpose:** Should only be used for genuine emergencies.

3. **Adequate Size:** Should cover at least 3–6 months of essential living expenses.

8.2 Why You Need an Emergency Fund?

1. Protection from Financial Setbacks

Emergencies such as job loss, medical bills, or urgent home repairs can happen at any time. Without a financial buffer, you may have to rely on credit cards or loans, which can lead to long-term debt.

2. Peace of Mind

Knowing you have funds to manage the unexpected reduces stress and helps you focus on other aspects of your life.

3. Prevents Disruptions in Financial Goals

An emergency fund ensures you don't need to dip into your savings, retirement accounts, or investments to cover unforeseen expenses.

4. Helps Avoid High-Interest Debt

Without a safety net, people often resort to credit cards or payday loans, which come with exorbitant interest rates.

8.3 How Much Should You Save?

General Rule of Thumb

- Save **3–6 months** of essential living expenses.

Factors to Consider

1. **Income Stability:**

   - If you have a stable job, aim for 3 months.

   - Freelancers or those with variable income should aim for 6–12 months.

2. **Dependents:**

   - More dependents mean a higher emergency fund is necessary.

3. **Health Status:**

   - If you have recurring medical expenses, save more.

4. **Debt Levels:**

   - If you have significant debt, an emergency fund becomes even more critical.

Start Small

- Set an initial goal of $500–$1,000 to cover minor emergencies, then build toward your target amount.

8.4 How to Build an Emergency Fund?

Step 1: Assess Your Monthly Expenses

- Identify essential expenses, including:

    o Rent or mortgage.

    o Utilities.

    o Groceries.

    o Transportation.

    o Insurance premiums.

Step 2: Set a Savings Goal

- Multiply your monthly essential expenses by the number of months you want to cover (e.g., 6 months).

- **Example:**

    o Monthly essential expenses: $2,000

    o Savings goal: $2,000 × 6 = $12,000

Step 3: Create a Savings Plan

- **Start with a Budget:** Reallocate funds from non-essential expenses to savings.

- **Automate Savings:** Set up automatic transfers to your emergency fund account.

- **Increase Savings Gradually:** Start with small contributions and increase them as your income grows.

Step 4: Supplement with Extra Income

- Use bonuses, tax refunds, or windfalls to boost your fund.

- Take on a side hustle or sell unused items to accelerate savings.

Step 5: Keep It Separate

- Open a dedicated savings or money market account for your emergency fund.

- Avoid mixing it with your regular checking or savings account.

8.5 Where to Keep Your Emergency Fund?

1. High-Yield Savings Account

- Offers easy access and earns interest over time.
- **Pros:** Liquidity, safety, and minimal fees.
- **Cons:** Lower returns compared to investments.

2. Money Market Account

- Like a savings account but may offer higher interest rates.
- **Pros:** Safe, accessible, and slightly better returns.
- **Cons:** May require a higher minimum balance.

3. Certificates of Deposit (CDs)

- Locks in your money for a set term with a higher interest rate.
- **Pros:** Better returns if you don't need immediate access.
- **Cons:** Penalties for early withdrawal.

4. Cash

- Keep a small portion in cash for immediate emergencies.
- **Pros:** Instant availability.
- **Cons:** No interest and risk of loss.

8.6 When to Use Your Emergency Fund?

An emergency fund should only be used for **genuine emergencies**, such as:

1. **Medical Emergencies:** Unexpected bills, surgeries, or treatments.
2. **Job Loss:** Covering essential expenses while unemployed.
3. **Urgent Repairs:** Car breakdowns or home repairs like a leaking roof.
4. **Family Emergencies:** Travel for an unforeseen family crisis.

When NOT to Use It?

- Planned expenses (vacations, holidays).

- Non-essential purchases (gadgets, entertainment).

- Paying off debt (this should come from your regular budget).

8.7 Replenishing Your Emergency Fund

1. Prioritize Rebuilding

- As soon as you use your fund, create a plan to rebuild it.

2. Adjust Your Budget

- Temporarily reduce discretionary spending to replenish the fund faster.

3. Use Windfalls

- Apply bonuses, tax refunds, or unexpected income directly to your fund.

8.8 Common Challenges and Solutions

Challenge 1: Difficulty Saving

- **Solution:** Start small and automate savings. Even $20 a week adds up over time.

Challenge 2: Temptation to Spend

- **Solution:** Keep your fund in a separate account to reduce easy access.

Challenge 3: Balancing Debt Repayment

- **Solution:** Split your focus between building a small emergency fund (e.g., $1,000) and paying down high-interest debt.

8.9 Emergency Fund vs. Other Savings

Emergency Fund vs. Rainy-Day Fund

- **Emergency Fund:** Covers major, unexpected expenses.

- **Rainy-Day Fund:** Covers smaller, more frequent surprises (e.g., minor car repairs).

Emergency Fund vs. Investments

- **Emergency Fund:** Safe, liquid, and not exposed to market risks.

- **Investments:** Higher returns but less accessible and more volatile.

Rule: Build an emergency fund before investing aggressively.

8.10 Building Long-Term Resilience

1. **Incorporate Savings as a Habit:** Treat your emergency fund contributions like a monthly bill.

2. **Periodically Reassess Needs:** Update your target amount as your expenses and life circumstances change.

3. **Educate Family Members:** Ensure everyone understands the purpose of the fund and avoids misusing it.

End of Chapter 8: Key Takeaways

1. An emergency fund provides financial security and reduces reliance on debt.

2. Aim to save 3–6 months of essential living expenses, starting with a smaller, manageable goal.

3. Keep your fund in a safe, accessible account, such as a high-yield savings account.

4. Use your funds only for genuine emergencies and replenish it as soon as possible.

Treat your emergency fund as a critical component of your overall financial plan.

Chapter 9: Building Wealth Through Real Estate

Real estate has long been a popular wealth-building tool due to its potential to generate both passive income and long-term appreciation. Unlike other investment vehicles, real estate offers tangible assets that can serve as both a home and an investment. However, real estate investing also comes with challenges, including market fluctuations, management responsibilities, and upfront costs.

This chapter provides an in-depth guide to understanding real estate as an investment, the different strategies available, how to get started, and best practices to build wealth through real estate.

9.1 Why Real Estate Is a Powerful Investment Tool

1. Tangible Asset

- Real estate is a physical asset you can see and use, providing a sense of security compared to intangible investments like stocks.

2. Multiple Income Streams

- Real estate can generate rental income while appreciating in value over time.

3. Hedge Against Inflation

- Property values and rents often rise with inflation, protecting your purchasing power.

4. Leverage

- Real estate allows you to use leverage (borrowed money) to buy properties, amplifying your potential returns.

5. Tax Benefits

- Investors can benefit from tax deductions on mortgage interest, property taxes, and depreciation.

6. Portfolio Diversification

- Adding real estate to your investment portfolio reduces overall risk by spreading your assets across different classes.

9.2 Types of Real Estate Investments

1. Residential Properties

- Includes single-family homes, apartments, and vacation rentals.

- Typically rented out to tenants for monthly income.

- Ideal for beginners due to familiarity and high demand.

2. Commercial Properties

- Includes office spaces, retail stores, warehouses, and industrial buildings.

- Tenants are businesses, often offering long-term lease agreements and higher returns.

- Requires significant capital and experience.

3. Real Estate Investment Trusts (REITs)

- REITs are companies that own, operate, or finance income-generating real estate.

- Investors buy shares and earn dividends without owning physical property.

- Highly liquid and accessible with minimal capital.

4. Vacation Rentals

- Short-term rental properties listed on platforms like Airbnb or Vrbo.

- Can generate higher income than traditional rentals but require active management.

5. Land

- Investing in undeveloped land for future use or resale.

- Profits depend on location and development potential.

6. Real Estate Crowdfunding

- Platforms allow individuals to pool funds for large real estate projects.
- Offers fractional ownership and lower entry barriers.

9.3 How to Get Started in Real Estate Investing?

Step 1: Educate Yourself

- Learn the basics of real estate investing, including market trends, financing options, and property management.
- Books like *Rich Dad Poor Dad* and *The Millionaire Real Estate Investor* are excellent starting points.

Step 2: Set Your Goals

- Define your objectives:
    - Passive income through rentals?
    - Long-term appreciation?
    - Diversification of investments?

Step 3: Assess Your Financial Readiness

- Build an emergency fund and pay down high-interest debts before investing.
- Ensure you have enough savings for a down payment and property-related costs.

Step 4: Choose a Market

- Research locations with strong demand, economic growth, and population increases.
- Factors to consider include:
    - Job opportunities.
    - Quality of schools and infrastructure.
    - Crime rates and amenities.

Step 5: Secure Financing

- Common financing options include:
    - **Mortgages:** Fixed or variable rates.
    - **Hard Money Loans:** Short-term, higher-interest loans for quick acquisitions.
    - **HELOCs (Home Equity Lines of Credit):** Using equity in your home for down payments.

Step 6: Start Small

- Begin with a single property or REIT investment to gain experience without overcommitting financially.

Step 7: Conduct Due Diligence

- Inspect the property thoroughly for structural issues or legal complications.

- Analyse cash flow potential by calculating:
    - Monthly rent vs. operating expenses (mortgage, taxes, insurance, maintenance).

9.4 Real Estate Investment Strategies

1. Buy-and-Hold

- Purchase a property, rent it out, and hold it for long-term appreciation.

- Best for steady income and building equity over time.

2. Flipping

- Buy undervalued properties, renovate them, and sell for a profit.

- High potential returns but requires significant expertise and capital.

3. House Hacking

- Live in one unit of a multi-family property while renting out the others.

- Reduces your housing costs while building equity.

4. BRRRR Method

- Buy, Rehab, Rent, Refinance, Repeat.

- A strategy to scale your portfolio by reinvesting equity from one property into another.

5. Real Estate Syndication

- Partner with other investors to pool resources for large-scale projects.

- Passive investment where syndicators manage the property.

6. Vacation Rentals

- Maximize income from short-term tenants.

- Requires location-specific expertise and active property management.

9.5 Managing Rental Properties

1. Screening Tenants

- Check credit scores, income stability, and rental history to reduce risks.

2. Setting the Right Rent

- Analyse market rates to ensure competitiveness without undervaluing your property.

3. Maintenance and Repairs

- Regular upkeep ensures property value and tenant satisfaction.

4. Outsourcing Management

- Hire property management companies to handle rent collection, tenant communication, and maintenance, especially for multiple properties.

9.6 Risks in Real Estate Investing

1. Market Fluctuations

- Real estate markets can crash, reducing property values.

- Mitigate risk by choosing stable markets and holding properties long-term.

2. Vacancy Risk

- Empty units lead to lost income while expenses continue.

- Reduce risk by investing in high-demand areas and maintaining properties well.

3. Legal and Regulatory Issues

- Landlord-tenant laws and zoning regulations can complicate investments.

- Stay informed about local laws to avoid penalties.

4. Leverage Risk

- Borrowing amplifies both gains and losses.

- Avoid overleveraging by keeping a manageable debt-to-equity ratio.

5. Liquidity Challenges

- Real estate is not as liquid as stocks or bonds, making it harder to sell quickly during emergencies.

9.7 Tax Benefits for Real Estate Investors

1. Depreciation

- Deduct a portion of the property's value annually as a non-cash expense

2. Mortgage Interest Deduction

- Deduct interest paid on loans for rental properties.

3. Capital Gains Tax

- Pay reduced taxes on long-term gains from property sales.

4. 1031 Exchange

- Defer taxes by reinvesting proceeds from a property sale into a similar investment.

9.8 Scaling Your Real Estate Portfolio

1. Reinvest Earnings

- Use profits from one property to acquire more assets.

2. Leverage Equity

- Refinance properties to extract equity for future purchases.

3. Partner with Others

- Pool resources with like-minded investors to scale faster.

9.9 Common Mistakes to Avoid

1. **Lack of Research:** Buying in the wrong market can lead to poor returns.

2. **Underestimating Costs:** Ignoring maintenance, taxes, and vacancy expenses.

3. **Overleveraging:** Borrowing too much can result in financial stress.

4. **Skipping Inspections:** Structural issues can lead to unexpected costs.

End of Chapter 9: Key Takeaways

1. Real estate offers diverse opportunities for income and growth.

2. Start with a clear goal, adequate financing, and a solid understanding of the market.

3. Choose the strategy that aligns with your resources and risk tolerance.

4. Manage risks through diversification, due diligence, and proper tenant screening.

Scale your portfolio strategically for long-term wealth building.

Chapter 10: Achieving Financial Freedom

Financial freedom is the ultimate goal for many individuals—it's about having the resources, flexibility, and peace of mind to live life on your terms. It means being free from the constant worry of money, having the ability to pursue your passions, and securing your future without depending on others or external circumstances.

In this chapter, we'll dive deep into the principles, steps, and habits required to achieve financial freedom. Whether you're starting your journey, midway through, or nearing your goal, this chapter provides actionable insights to guide you.

10.1 What is Financial Freedom?

Definition

Financial freedom is the state of having sufficient wealth and income to cover your living expenses without actively working for money.

Key Characteristics of Financial Freedom:

1. **No Debt:** You're free from financial obligations such as credit card debt, student loans, and mortgages.

2. **Emergency Preparedness:** You have a robust emergency fund to handle unforeseen expenses.

3. **Multiple Income Streams:** You rely on diverse sources of income, including passive income.

4. **Work by Choice:** You work because you enjoy it, not because you have to.

5. **Financial Security:** Your investments and savings generate enough income to sustain your lifestyle.

10.2 The Pillars of Financial Freedom

Achieving financial freedom requires a solid foundation built on the following pillars:

1. Clear Financial Goals

- Define what financial freedom means to you. It might include early retirement, travelling the world, or starting a business.

- Use the SMART framework to set goals:
    - **Specific:** What do you want to achieve?
    - **Measurable:** How much money do you need?
    - **Achievable:** Is it realistic based on your current situation?
    - **Relevant:** Does it align with your values?
    - **Time-Bound:** By when do you want to achieve it?

2. Budgeting and Expense Management

- Create a budget that aligns with your financial goals.

- Use the **50/30/20 Rule**:
    - 50% for necessities (housing, food, utilities).
    - 30% for discretionary spending (entertainment, hobbies).
    - 20% for savings and debt repayment.

Tools for Budgeting:

- Budgeting apps like Mint, YNAB (You Need a Budget), or Excel spreadsheets.

3. Debt Elimination

Debt is often the biggest obstacle to financial freedom.

- **Strategies to Eliminate Debt:**
    - **Debt Snowball Method:** Pay off the smallest debts first for quick wins, then tackle larger ones.
    - **Debt Avalanche Method:** Focus on high-interest debts first to save money on interest.

4. Saving and Investing

- Automate savings to ensure consistency.

- Build an emergency fund with 3–6 months of living expenses.

- Invest in diversified assets such as stocks, bonds, real estate, and mutual funds.

Compounding:

- The earlier you start, the more you benefit from compound interest. For example, investing $10,000 at an 8% annual return grows to over $46,000 in 20 years.

5. Multiple Income Streams

- Diversify income sources to reduce reliance on a single paycheck.

- Explore options like:

  - **Passive Income:** Rental properties, dividends, royalties.

  - **Side Hustles:** Freelancing, consulting, or selling products.

  - **Business Ventures:** Entrepreneurship for long-term wealth building.

10.3 Steps to Achieve Financial Freedom

Step 1: Assess Your Current Financial Situation

- Analyse your net worth:

  - **Net Worth = Total Assets - Total Liabilities**

- Track income, expenses, debts, and investments.

Step 2: Create a Financial Freedom Plan

- Break your goal into smaller milestones, such as paying off debt, saving an emergency fund, or reaching investment targets.

Step 3: Increase Your Income

- Negotiate for higher pay at your current job.

- Acquire new skills or certifications to boost earning potential.

- Start side hustles or small businesses for additional income streams.

Step 4: Reduce Expenses

- Differentiate between needs and wants.

- Downsize or adopt a minimalist lifestyle to save more.

- Cut unnecessary subscriptions and optimize spending habits.

Step 5: Focus on Investing

- Prioritize long-term investments over short-term gains.

- Follow an asset allocation strategy that matches your risk tolerance.

- Reinvest returns to accelerate growth.

Step 6: Protect Your Wealth

- Obtain adequate insurance (health, life, property, and liability).

- Create an estate plan to ensure your assets are managed and transferred according to your wishes.

10.4 Overcoming Obstacles to Financial Freedom

1. Emotional Spending

- Avoid impulse purchases by waiting 24 hours before buying.

- Use cash or debit cards instead of credit cards to limit overspending.

2. Fear of Investing

- Educate yourself on investment basics.

- Start small and gradually increase your investments as you gain confidence.

- Consult a financial advisor if needed.

3. Procrastination

- Break large goals into smaller, actionable steps.

- Set deadlines and hold yourself accountable.

10.5 The Role of Passive Income

Passive income is a cornerstone of financial freedom. It is money earned with minimal ongoing effort.

Examples of Passive Income Sources:

- **Real Estate:** Rental properties or REITs (Real Estate Investment Trusts).

- **Investments:** Dividends, interest, and capital gains.

- **Digital Products:** E-books, courses, or apps.

- **Royalties:** Income from intellectual property like books, music, or patents.

10.6 Maintaining Financial Freedom

Achieving financial freedom is one thing; maintaining it is another.

1. Regular Financial Reviews

- Assess your financial progress every six months or annually.

- Adjust your plan as life circumstances change.

2. Avoid Lifestyle Inflation

- Resist the urge to spend more as your income grows.

- Focus on long-term goals instead of short-term pleasures.

3. Continuous Learning

- Stay informed about personal finance, investing, and economic trends.

- Take courses or read books to enhance financial literacy.

10.7 Real-Life Examples of Financial Freedom

Case 1: The Frugal Investor

- A young professional saved 50% of their income, invested in index funds, and achieved financial freedom by 40.

Case 2: The Passive Income Strategist

- A couple built a real estate portfolio and diversified into dividend-paying stocks, enabling them to retire early and travel full-time.

End of Chapter 10: Key Takeaways

1. Financial freedom is about independence, security, and the ability to live life on your terms.

2. Build a strong foundation with budgeting, saving, and investing.

3. Diversify income sources and focus on passive income to accelerate your journey.

4. Protect your wealth through insurance, estate planning, and disciplined spending.

Regularly review and adapt your financial plan to stay on track.

Chapter 11: Cultivating an Abundance Mindset

An abundance mindset is the foundation of lasting financial success and overall personal growth. It's the belief that there are ample opportunities in life and that you can achieve your financial goals without scarcity or competition. By shifting from a scarcity mindset, which focuses on lack and limitations, to an abundance mindset, you open yourself to possibilities, wealth creation, and prosperity. This chapter will explore the power of the abundance mindset, how to develop it, and how it can positively influence your financial journey.

11.1 What is an Abundance Mindset?

An abundance mindset is the belief that there is enough wealth, success, love, and happiness for everyone. People with this mindset focus on opportunities, collaboration, and growth. They view challenges as opportunities for learning and see the success of others as something to be celebrated, not feared or envied.

Key Characteristics of an Abundance Mindset

- **Optimism:** Belief that positive change and growth are always possible.

- **Generosity:** Willingness to share resources and help others succeed.

- **Growth-Oriented:** Focus on personal development and continuous learning.

- **Gratitude:** Acknowledging and appreciating what you already have while being open to receiving more.

- **Non-competitive:** Understanding that another person's success does not diminish your own potential.

11.2 The Power of an Abundance Mindset

Having an abundance mindset empowers you to pursue your goals with a sense of possibility and confidence. This mindset affects not just your financial decisions, but also how you approach career development, relationships, and personal well-being.

How an Abundance Mindset Transforms Your Financial Journey?

- **Encourages Risk-Taking:** You are more likely to invest, start a business, or pursue new ventures without fear of losing everything.

- **Opens Opportunities:** You recognize opportunities that others may miss because you are open-minded and adaptable.

- **Promotes Wealth Creation:** You believe that wealth can be created in many forms, whether through investments, business, or collaborations.

- **Enhances Networking and Collaboration:** You value working with others, fostering partnerships that lead to mutual growth.

11.3 Scarcity vs. Abundance Mindset

Scarcity Mindset

People with a scarcity mindset believe that resources—whether money, time, or opportunities—are limited. They tend to be fearful, competitive, and protective of their assets. They may hold onto money tightly and avoid risks, believing that any loss is irreparable.

Key Traits of a Scarcity Mindset:

- **Fear of Loss:** You focus on what could go wrong and avoid taking risks.

- **Jealousy:** You compare yourself to others and feel resentment over their success.

- **Fixed View of Resources:** You believe that money, opportunities, and success are finite.

- **Defensiveness:** You are reluctant to share knowledge, opportunities, or resources, believing that someone else's success diminishes your own.

Abundance Mindset

In contrast, those with an abundance mindset believe that the world is full of opportunities. They trust that there is enough for everyone and that their success does not depend on someone else's failure. This mindset fosters creativity, collaboration, and generosity.

Key Traits of an Abundance Mindset:

- **Opportunity Focused:** You see setbacks as opportunities for growth and learning.

- **Generosity:** You willingly share knowledge, resources, and support with others.

- **Long-Term Vision:** You focus on creating lasting wealth, not short-term gains.

- **Adaptability:** You are open to change and view it as a chance for improvement.

11.4 Developing an Abundance Mindset

1. Shift Your Perspective

- **Identify and Challenge Limiting Beliefs:** Replace thoughts like "I'll never have enough money" with "There's plenty of wealth to be made, and I can create it."

- **Focus on Possibilities, Not Problems:** When faced with challenges, think about potential solutions and opportunities instead of focusing on limitations.

2. Practice Gratitude

- **Daily Gratitude Journaling:** Write down things you are thankful for every day, especially related to your financial life (e.g., a steady income, family support, or financial growth).

- **Celebrating Success:** Acknowledge and celebrate even small victories in your financial journey.

3. Build Positive Financial Habits

- **Consistency Over Perfection:** Focus on making regular, steady progress, rather than trying to make perfect financial decisions.

- **Invest in Self-Education:** Read books, attend seminars, or take courses to increase your financial literacy.

- **Focus on Long-Term Goals:** Avoid chasing quick fixes and instead invest in long-term financial health.

4. Surround Yourself with Abundant Thinkers

- **Networking with Like-Minded People:** Spend time with people who believe in abundance and who support your growth.

- **Learn from the Success of Others:** Celebrate and learn from others' achievements, rather than comparing yourself to them.

5. Embrace Giving and Sharing

- **Give Back:** Whether through charity, mentorship, or helping others in your community, giving can amplify the abundance you feel in your life.

- **Create Win-Win Situations:** Look for opportunities to create value for others while achieving your own goals.

11.5 Practical Applications of an Abundance Mindset in Personal Finance

An abundance mindset doesn't just influence your attitude—it can change the way you make financial decisions.

1. Budgeting and Saving with Optimism

- **Create a Flexible Budget:** Rather than restricting yourself too much, build a budget that allows for growth, investments, and enjoying life.

- **Save with Purpose:** Save for goals that excite and inspire you, such as travel, buying a home, or funding an entrepreneurial project.

2. Investing with Confidence

- **Long-Term Investment Strategy:** With an abundance mindset, you're not afraid to make long-term investments in stocks, bonds, real estate, or businesses that will grow over time.

- **Invest in Yourself:** Attend workshops, invest in your education, and develop skills that enhance your earning potential.

3. Setting Financial Goals

- **Aim High:** When you set goals, make them ambitious yet achievable. Trust in your ability to reach them by developing a strategic plan.

- **Be Open to Multiple Sources of Wealth:** You don't have to rely on a single income source. Create a mix of active and passive income streams to diversify your financial portfolio.

4. Dealing with Financial Setbacks

- **Learn and Move Forward:** View setbacks as learning experiences. Instead of panicking, ask yourself, "What can I learn from this?"

- **Stay Focused on Growth:** Keep your eyes on your long-term goals, and keep moving forward with incremental steps, even during tough times.

11.6 The Role of Gratitude and Positive Thinking

Gratitude and positive thinking are fundamental to developing an abundance mindset. Studies have shown that people who practice gratitude tend to experience lower levels of stress, higher levels of happiness, and even improved financial outcomes.

How Gratitude Enhances Financial Success?

- **Shifts Focus from Lack to Abundance:** When you are thankful for what you have, it helps you feel more abundant, which in turn attracts more prosperity into your life.

- **Promotes a Healthy Relationship with Money:** Viewing money as a tool to help you and others can shift your perspective from anxiety to appreciation.

- **Boosts Resilience:** Gratitude helps you maintain a positive attitude, even in the face of financial challenges, making it easier to bounce back.

11.7 Overcoming Challenges with an Abundance Mindset

1. Fear of Financial Failure

- Instead of fearing failure, use it as motivation to learn. Each financial mistake teaches you valuable lessons for future success.

2. Competition and Envy

- Celebrate others' successes rather than comparing yourself to them. Abundance doesn't diminish—it multiplies.

3. Dealing with Financial Pressure

- Trust that challenges are temporary and that your efforts will eventually pay off.

End of Chapter 11: Key Takeaways

1. An abundance mindset fosters growth, collaboration, and creativity, which are key to financial success.

2. A scarcity mindset limits opportunities, stifles creativity, and can lead to financial stagnation.

3. Developing an abundance mindset involves practising gratitude, focusing on opportunities, and surrounding yourself with positive influences.

4. Embrace giving, learn from others' successes, and invest in your personal and financial growth.

By applying the principles of an abundance mindset, you'll not only improve your financial situation but also enhance your overall life satisfaction.

Chapter 12: Personal Finance Myths and Misconceptions

Personal finance is an area where many people struggle due to misconceptions and myths that can distort financial decision-making. Whether it's about budgeting, investing, saving, or debt management, these myths can mislead individuals into making poor choices that hurt their financial future. In this chapter, we will debunk common personal finance myths, provide clarity on these issues, and offer guidance on how to make sound financial decisions that will set you on the path to financial success.

12.1 Myth 1: "You Need a High Income to Build Wealth"

One of the most pervasive myths about personal finance is that wealth is only achievable if you have a high-paying job or a substantial income. While a high income can certainly accelerate your path to wealth, it's not the only factor. In fact, many people who earn modest salaries manage to build significant wealth by living below their means, saving aggressively, and investing wisely.

Why This Myth Is False?

- **Wealth is Built Over Time, Not Overnight:** Building wealth is a long-term process. Even if your income is not particularly high, consistent saving and smart investing can lead to wealth accumulation over time.

- **Living Below Your Means is Key:** Regardless of your income, the real secret to building wealth lies in managing your expenses. By spending less than you earn, you create the room to save and invest.

- **The Power of Compound Interest:** When you invest early, even small amounts, compound interest can make a huge difference. The longer your money has to grow, the more wealth you can accumulate, regardless of your starting point.

Action Steps:

- Focus on increasing your savings rate, not just your income.

- Build multiple streams of income—consider side hustles, investments, or business ventures.

- Start investing early, even if it's a small amount, to take advantage of compounding growth.

12.2 Myth 2: "Debt is Always Bad"

Debt is often viewed negatively in personal finance circles, but not all debt is bad. The key difference lies in how you use debt. Some forms of debt can actually be a tool for wealth building, while others can hold you back financially.

Why This Myth Is False?

- **Good Debt vs. Bad Debt:** Not all debt is created equal. "Good debt" refers to debt that helps you invest in assets that appreciate in value, such as a mortgage or student loan. "Bad debt" is high-interest debt that does not create value, like credit card debt or payday loans.

- **Leverage Can Be Beneficial:** In some cases, using debt strategically can amplify your wealth-building efforts. For example, taking out a mortgage to buy property, or using student loans to obtain an education that increases your earning potential, can be considered good debt.

- **The Problem with Bad Debt:** Bad debt, especially high-interest debt, can be financially draining. It prevents you from saving and investing, often leading to a vicious cycle of borrowing to pay off past borrowing.

Action Steps:

- Distinguish between good and bad debt and focus on using debt strategically to build wealth.

- Pay off high-interest debt quickly to avoid it draining your finances.

- If you need to borrow, ensure that the debt serves a purpose and contributes to your long-term financial goals.

12.3 Myth 3: "You Should Avoid All Risks in Investing"

Many people shy away from investing because they believe it's too risky or because they've heard that they should only invest in "safe" assets like bonds or savings accounts. While investing carries risks, avoiding all risks may limit your wealth-building potential.

Why This Myth Is False?

- **All Investments Carry Some Risk:** Every investment, from stocks to bonds to real estate, carries some level of risk. However, the risk is often associated with the potential for higher returns. The key is to understand your risk tolerance and diversify your investments.

- **Risk vs. Reward:** Historically, higher-risk investments like stocks have outperformed lower-risk assets like bonds over the long term. To build wealth, it's essential to take on some risk—especially if you're investing for long-term goals like retirement.

- **The Importance of Diversification:** Diversification is one of the best ways to manage risk. By spreading your investments across different asset classes (stocks, bonds, real estate, etc.), you reduce the risk of any one investment negatively impacting your portfolio.

Action Steps:

- Assess your risk tolerance and develop a diversified investment strategy that matches your financial goals and time horizon.

- Understand that short-term market fluctuations are normal—invest for the long-term and avoid making emotional decisions.

- Consider consulting with a financial advisor to help manage risk and create a balanced portfolio.

12.4 Myth 4: "You Should Focus Only on Cutting Expenses to Save"

Many financial experts focus on the importance of cutting expenses as a way to save money. While reducing unnecessary expenses is important, it's not the only way to build wealth. Focusing too much on cutting costs can lead to a restrictive mindset and limit your financial potential.

Why This Myth Is False?

- **Income Growth is Just as Important:** Instead of just slashing your expenses, you should also focus on growing your income. This might involve pursuing a career promotion, starting a side business, or investing in education or training to increase your earning potential.

- **The 80/20 Rule:** It's often more effective to focus on the 20% of your expenses that consume 80% of your budget (e.g., housing, transportation, and food) rather than nickel-and-diming every small purchase.

- **Enjoying Life While Saving:** A good financial plan allows for both saving and spending. You don't need to deprive yourself of enjoyable experiences in order to save money.

Action Steps:

- Find ways to increase your income, such as through a side hustle or skill development.

- Make sure you're managing your biggest expenses (housing, transportation, etc.) in the most cost-effective way.

- Create a budget that balances saving and enjoying life—ensure you can still spend on things that bring you joy while building wealth.

12.5 Myth 5: "You Should Pay Off Your Mortgage as Quickly as Possible"

Paying off your mortgage early is often considered a sign of financial prudence. However, in many cases, it may not be the best financial strategy.

Why This Myth Is False?

- **Opportunity Cost:** The money you put toward paying off your mortgage could potentially be invested elsewhere for higher returns. For example, if your mortgage interest rate is low (e.g., 3-4%) and the stock market historically provides higher returns, you might be better off investing your extra money.

- **Liquidity and Flexibility:** Having a fully paid-off home doesn't provide you with liquidity or flexibility. You may be better off keeping a mortgage and using extra funds to invest in assets that offer higher returns or provide emergency cash flow.

- **Tax Benefits:** In some cases, mortgage interest is tax-deductible. By keeping your mortgage and investing the extra money elsewhere, you may benefit from tax deductions and compounding investment returns.

Action Steps:

- Evaluate whether paying off your mortgage early is the best use of your extra money, based on your interest rate and potential investment returns.

- Consider keeping a mortgage and using the additional funds to invest in assets with a higher return potential.

- If your mortgage interest rate is high or you have financial goals that require liquidity, paying off your mortgage sooner might still be the right choice.

12.6 Myth 6: "Credit Cards are Always Bad"

Credit cards often get a bad reputation due to the potential for high interest rates and debt accumulation. However, when used responsibly, credit cards can be a valuable tool in managing finances and even earning rewards.

Why This Myth Is False?

- **Building Credit History:** Responsible use of credit cards can help you build a strong credit history, which is important for obtaining favourable terms on loans and mortgages.

- **Rewards and Perks:** Many credit cards offer rewards programs, cashback, and travel perks. When paid off in full each month, these rewards can be a wonderful way to get more value from your spending.

- **Flexibility and Security:** Credit cards offer flexibility in managing cash flow and often come with fraud protection, which adds an extra layer of security.

Action Steps:

- Use credit cards wisely by paying off balances in full each month to avoid high-interest charges.

- Take advantage of rewards programs and cashback offers to get the most out of your spending.

- Keep track of your credit card usage and ensure that it's helping, not hindering, your financial goals.

End of Chapter 12: Key Takeaways

1. **Income isn't the only key to wealth.** It's about how much you save, invest, and how strategically you manage your money.

2. **Not all debt is bad.** Use debt responsibly to leverage opportunities that build wealth but avoid high-interest debt.

3. **Investing involves risk,** but it's necessary for wealth accumulation. Diversification is essential to manage risk effectively.

4. **Cutting expenses is important,** but growing your income is equally crucial in building long-term wealth.

5. **Paying off your mortgage early** might not always be the best financial strategy if better investment opportunities exist.

6. **Credit cards can be useful** if used responsibly building credit, earning rewards, and providing security.

Chapter 13: Building a Solid Financial Future: Long-Term Strategies

Building wealth is not an overnight endeavour—it's the result of consistent effort, smart decision-making, and long-term planning. In this chapter, we will focus on the long-term strategies that can set the foundation for a secure financial future. From creating a comprehensive financial plan to establishing multiple streams of income and preparing for retirement, these strategies will help you build lasting wealth and achieve your financial goals.

13.1 Creating a Comprehensive Financial Plan

A financial plan is a blueprint for your financial future. It outlines your financial goals, maps out the steps needed to achieve them, and helps you stay on track. A well-thought-out financial plan should be tailored to your circumstances and consider your income, expenses, assets, liabilities, and future goals.

Key Components of a Financial Plan:

1. **Income Assessment:** Start by understanding your current income sources. This includes your salary, business income, investments, and any other streams of income. Establishing a clear picture of how much money you earn will guide your budgeting and saving efforts.

2. **Expense Tracking:** Keep track of your monthly expenses to identify areas where you can cut back. Categorize your spending into fixed expenses (e.g., rent, utilities) and discretionary spending (e.g., dining out, entertainment). Use a budgeting tool or app to stay organized.

3. **Debt Management Plan:** If you have debt, develop a strategy for paying it off. Focus on high-interest debt first (e.g., credit card debt) while making minimum payments on other loans. Consider consolidating or refinancing debt if it helps reduce interest rates.

4. **Emergency Fund:** Building an emergency fund should be a priority in your financial plan. An emergency fund should cover 3-6 months of living expenses to protect you in case of unexpected events such as job loss or medical emergencies.

5. **Savings and Investments:** Determine your savings goals and choose the right investment vehicles. Investments should align with your time horizon, risk tolerance, and financial goals. Start with retirement accounts like 401(k)s and IRAs, and consider additional investments such as stocks, bonds, and real estate.

6. **Insurance Coverage:** Insurance is an essential component of financial planning. It protects you from monetary loss in case of accidents, illness, or property damage. Ensure that you have adequate health, life, auto, and home insurance coverage.

7. **Estate Planning:** Estate planning involves organizing your assets and making plans for their distribution after your death. This may include creating a will, establishing trusts, and appointing beneficiaries for your accounts.

How to Create Your Financial Plan?

- **Step 1:** Set clear financial goals. These should be specific, measurable, achievable, relevant, and time-bound (SMART goals).

- **Step 2:** Assess your current financial situation. List all your assets, liabilities, income, and expenses.

- **Step 3:** Develop a savings and investment strategy. Choose the right mix of investment vehicles to reach your goals.

- **Step 4:** Revisit your plan regularly. Adjust your goals and strategies as your financial situation changes over time.

13.2 Establishing Multiple Streams of Income

Relying on a single source of income can be risky, especially in uncertain economic times. By establishing multiple streams of income, you can reduce financial stress, improve your cash flow, and accelerate wealth-building. Multiple income sources can come from your primary job, side businesses, investments, or freelance work.

Types of Income Streams:

1. **Earned Income:** This is the money you make from your primary job or business. It's typically your most consistent source of income but can be limited by your working hours and salary.

2. **Investment Income:** This includes dividends from stocks, interest from bonds, rental income from real estate, and any other income earned from investments. Investment income is crucial for long-term wealth-building because it can generate passive income over time.

3. **Side Hustles:** A side hustle is a part-time business or freelance work that generates additional income. Popular side hustles include freelance writing, graphic design, tutoring, consulting, and online businesses. Side hustles offer flexibility and the potential to scale.

4. **Royalties and Residual Income:** If you have intellectual property, such as books, music, or patents, you can earn royalties. These are payments made to you for the use of your intellectual property. Similarly, residual income comes from products or services that continue to generate income after the initial effort is made.

5. **Rental Income:** Owning real estate properties and renting them out is a popular way to generate passive income. Rental properties can provide regular monthly income while also appreciating in value over time.

How to Build Multiple Streams of Income?

- **Start with what you know:** Leverage your skills, hobbies, or expertise to create a side business or offer freelance services.

- **Invest early:** Consider investing in stocks, real estate, or other assets that can generate passive income over time.

- **Diversify your investments:** Spread your investments across different sectors and asset classes to reduce risk.

- **Automate income:** Invest in income-producing assets like dividend-paying stocks, real estate, or royalties from intellectual property.

- **Scale your side hustles:** Once your side hustle becomes successful, look for ways to scale it, whether by increasing your workload, hiring help, or expanding into new markets.

13.3 Smart Tax Strategies for Long-Term Wealth

Taxes can take a significant chunk out of your earnings and savings, so it's important to develop smart tax strategies that minimize your tax burden and maximize your wealth-building potential. By using tax-advantaged accounts and understanding deductions and credits, you can reduce your taxable income and keep more of your hard-earned money.

Tax-Advantaged Accounts:

- **401(k) and 403(b):** These employer-sponsored retirement accounts allow you to contribute pre-tax income, reducing your taxable income for the year. The money in these accounts grows tax-deferred until retirement.

- **IRA (Individual Retirement Account):** IRAs come in two main types—Traditional and Roth. With a Traditional IRA, you can deduct your contributions from your taxable income, and the money grows tax deferred. With a Roth IRA, contributions are made with after-tax dollars, but withdrawals are tax-free in retirement.

- **HSA (Health Savings Account):** An HSA is a tax-advantaged account for healthcare expenses. Contributions are tax-deductible, the money grows tax-free, and withdrawals for qualified medical expenses are tax-free.

- **529 College Savings Plan:** If you're saving for a child's education, a 529 plan allows your contributions to grow tax-deferred, and withdrawals are tax-free when used for qualified education expenses.

Other Tax Strategies:

- **Maximize Deductions:** Take advantage of tax deductions, such as the mortgage interest deduction, student loan interest deduction, and charitable contributions. Keep detailed records to ensure you claim all eligible deductions.

- **Tax-Loss Harvesting:** If you have investments in taxable accounts, tax-loss harvesting can help you reduce your taxable income by selling investments that have lost value. The losses can offset gains from other investments, lowering your overall tax liability.

- **Capital Gains Strategies:** Long-term capital gains (on assets held for over a year) are taxed at a lower rate than short-term capital gains. If possible, hold investments for longer periods to take advantage of the lower tax rate.

How to Implement Tax Strategies?

- Contribute to tax-advantaged retirement accounts as much as possible.

- Consult with a tax professional to ensure you are taking advantage of all available tax breaks and deductions.

- Keep detailed records of your investments and business expenses to minimize your tax liability.

13.4 Planning for Retirement

Retirement may seem far off for some, but the earlier you start planning, the easier it will be to achieve financial independence. Saving for retirement requires more than just putting money into a 401(k)—it requires understanding your retirement goals, how much you need to save, and how to invest that money to ensure a comfortable retirement.

Key Considerations for Retirement Planning:

1. **Retirement Goals:** Start by determining what you want your retirement to look like. Do you plan to travel? Live in a different location? Pursue hobbies full-time? Understanding your goals will help you calculate how much money you need to save.

2. **Retirement Savings Estimates:** Use retirement calculators to estimate how much you need to save to meet your retirement goals. Consider factors like inflation, expected retirement age, and anticipated living expenses.

3. **Types of Retirement Accounts:** Contribute to employer-sponsored retirement accounts (such as a 401(k)) as well as individual accounts like IRAs. Understand the differences between Roth and Traditional IRAs and how each can benefit your retirement strategy.

4. **Investment Strategy for Retirement:** As you get closer to retirement, shift your investment strategy to a more conservative approach. However, it's important to continue investing in growth

assets (like stocks) to keep your money working for you during retirement.

5. **Social Security and Pension Plans:** Understand how Social Security benefits work and what you can expect to receive based on your earnings history. If you have a pension plan, learn how it works and estimate how much you will receive in retirement.

How to Plan for Retirement?

- Start saving as early as possible, even if it's a small amount.

- Use retirement calculators to determine your savings target.

- Review your retirement accounts regularly and adjust contributions as needed.

- Consider working with a financial planner to create a detailed retirement strategy.

End of Chapter 13: Key Takeaways

1. **Create a comprehensive financial plan** that outlines your goals and strategies for income, debt, savings, insurance, and estate planning.

2. **Establish multiple streams of income** to reduce risk and accelerate wealth-building through earned income, investments, side hustles, and royalties.

3. 3. **Use smart tax strategies** such as tax-advantaged accounts, deductions, and capital gains strategies to minimize your tax burden and maximize your wealth.

4. 4. **Plan for retirement** by setting clear goals, saving consistently, and making the right investment choices to ensure you can retire comfortably.

Chapter 14: Navigating Economic Uncertainty: Managing Your Finances During Turbulent Times

Economic uncertainty is an inevitable part of life, whether it's due to a market crash, a global recession, or unexpected personal circumstances. During turbulent times, maintaining financial stability and continuing to build wealth can seem challenging. However, with the right strategies and mindset, you can navigate through these difficult periods and emerge financially stronger.

In this chapter, we will discuss how to manage your finances effectively during economic downturns, build resilience to market volatility, and adopt a long-term perspective in uncertain times.

14.1 Understanding Economic Uncertainty

Economic uncertainty refers to periods when the future state of the economy is unpredictable. This can arise from various factors such as:

- **Market Crashes:** Stock market crashes or significant downturns in asset prices.

- **Recessions:** Economic slowdowns that impact employment, consumer spending, and business profits.

- **Inflation:** Rising prices for goods and services, which erode purchasing power.

- **Interest Rate Changes:** Central banks alter interest rates to control inflation or stimulate growth.

- **Global Events:** Natural disasters, geopolitical tensions, pandemics, or wars that disrupt economies.

While it's impossible to predict when economic uncertainty will occur, understanding the potential causes and impacts of these events will help you prepare for and manage your finances more effectively.

14.2 Building Financial Resilience

One of the keys to navigating economic uncertainty is building financial resilience. Financial resilience is the ability to absorb financial shocks and continue pursuing long-term financial goals despite temporary setbacks.

Key Strategies for Building Financial Resilience:

1. **Create an Emergency Fund:** An emergency fund is a safety net that allows you to cover unexpected expenses without relying on credit or loans. During uncertain times, having at least 3-6 months' worth of living expenses saved can help you weather financial storms.

2. **Diversify Your Investments:** Diversification reduces the risk of your portfolio by spreading your investments across different asset classes (stocks, bonds, real estate, etc.). In times of market volatility, some assets may perform better than others, so diversification can help stabilize your portfolio.

3. **Reduce Debt:** High levels of debt can create financial strain, particularly during uncertain economic times when income may be unpredictable. Focus on paying down high-interest debts and avoid taking on new debt unless absolutely necessary.

4. **Maintain Liquidity:** Having access to liquid assets—money or assets that can easily be converted to cash—ensures you can quickly respond to unexpected financial needs. Keep cash reserves in a savings account, money market fund, or other easily accessible options.

5. **Protect Your Income:** In uncertain times, job security may be at risk. Consider acquiring skills that increase your employability, diversifying your sources of income, or even building a side hustle that can help supplement your main income stream.

14.3 Adjusting Your Financial Strategy During a Recession

A recession is a period of economic decline, often characterized by higher unemployment, lower consumer spending, and reduced business investment. During a recession, your financial strategy may need to be adjusted to minimize risks and protect your financial well-being.

Financial Adjustments During a Recession:

1. **Reevaluate Your Spending Habits:** During a recession, it's important to scrutinize your spending and prioritize essential expenses. Cut back on discretionary spending (e.g., entertainment, dining out) and focus on saving and paying down debt.

2. **Rebalance Your Investment Portfolio:** A market downturn may prompt you to reassess your investment strategy. Consider reducing exposure to high-risk assets (such as stocks in volatile industries) and shifting to more conservative options (e.g., bonds or dividend-paying stocks).

3. **Avoid Panic Selling:** While it's natural to feel uneasy during a market downturn, avoid making emotional decisions. Panic selling can lock in losses. Instead, stay the course and focus on long-term goals. If possible, consider using dollar-cost averaging (DCA) to continue investing consistently over time, regardless of market conditions.

4. **Focus on Income-Producing Assets:** During a recession, it's beneficial to focus on investments that provide steady income, such as dividend stocks, real estate rental properties, or bonds. These income streams can help offset any volatility in your portfolio.

5. **Look for Opportunities:** Recessions can create opportunities to buy assets at discounted prices. If you have the liquidity, consider investing in stocks or real estate when they are undervalued. However, only do this if it aligns with your long-term investment strategy.

14.4 Coping with Inflation: Protecting Your Purchasing Power

Inflation occurs when the general price level of goods and services increases over time, reducing the purchasing power of money. When inflation is high, everyday expenses become more expensive, and your savings lose value. To protect your purchasing power during periods of high inflation, it's important to adopt strategies that preserve the value of your money.

Strategies for Coping with Inflation:

1. **Invest in Inflation-Protected Securities:** Certain types of investments are designed to protect against inflation. For example, Treasury Inflation-Protected Securities (TIPS) are government

bonds that increase in value with inflation, providing a hedge against rising prices.

2. **Diversify into Real Assets:** Real assets, such as real estate and commodities (e.g., gold, oil), tend to retain value during inflationary periods. Consider diversifying your portfolio to include these types of investments.

3. **Increase Income Streams:** To keep up with rising costs, look for ways to increase your income. This could involve asking for a raise, taking on additional work, or starting a side business.

4. **Cut Unnecessary Expenses:** Inflation often forces consumers to reexamine their spending. Focus on eliminating wasteful expenses (e.g., subscription services you don't use) and prioritize essentials.

5. **Focus on High-Quality Investments:** Quality investments that provide steady income, such as blue-chip stocks and real estate, may outperform other assets during inflationary times.

14.5 Navigating Market Volatility

Market volatility refers to the rapid and significant price fluctuations in the stock market or other financial markets. This can be caused by economic events, geopolitical instability, or investor sentiment. While volatility can create short-term losses, it can also offer opportunities for those who are prepared.

Strategies for Navigating Market Volatility:

1. **Adopt a Long-Term Perspective:** Volatility is typically short-term in nature. If you are investing for the long term (e.g., for retirement), market fluctuations should not disrupt your investment strategy. Stay focused on your goals and avoid making knee-jerk reactions.

2. **Dollar-Cost Averaging (DCA):** DCA involves investing a fixed amount of money regularly (e.g., monthly), regardless of market conditions. This strategy reduces the impact of short-term market fluctuations by spreading your investments over time.

3. **Keep Your Emergency Fund Intact:** In times of market volatility, it's important not to dip into your investment accounts to cover expenses. Maintain a robust emergency fund so that you can avoid selling investments in a down market.

4. **Rebalance Your Portfolio:** Periodically rebalance your investment portfolio to maintain your desired asset allocation. If certain assets have dropped in value, it may be an opportunity to buy them at a lower price.

5. **Avoid Timing the Market:** Trying to predict short-term market movements is nearly impossible and often leads to poor decisions. Instead, focus on long-term growth and consistent investing.

14.6 Preparing for Future Uncertainty

Economic uncertainty can be overwhelming, but the key to thriving during turbulent times is preparation. By adopting prudent financial strategies, building resilience, and staying informed, you can not only survive uncertain times but also position yourself for long-term success.

How to Prepare for Future Uncertainty?

1. **Stay Informed:** Keep up to date with economic news, market trends, and geopolitical developments. This allows you to make informed decisions about your finances and anticipate potential challenges.

2. **Review Your Financial Plan Regularly:** As economic conditions change, review, and adjust your financial plan to ensure it aligns with your current goals and circumstances.

3. **Diversify Your Income:** The more income streams you have, the less vulnerable you are to economic downturns. Build multiple sources of income to provide security in case one stream is disrupted.

4. **Continue Learning:** Financial education is a lifelong pursuit. Stay informed about personal finance, investing, and money management to ensure that you make the best decisions for your future.

End of Chapter 14: Key Takeaways

1. **Economic uncertainty is inevitable**, but with the right strategies, you can navigate through difficult times.

2. **Building financial resilience** through an emergency fund, diversified investments, and reduced debt is key to surviving market downturns.

3. **Adjusting your financial strategy** during a recession involves reevaluating spending, rebalancing investments, and focusing on income-producing assets.

4. **Coping with inflation** requires investing in inflation-protected securities, diversifying into real assets, and increasing income streams.

5. **Navigating market volatility** requires a long-term perspective, dollar-cost averaging, and rebalancing your portfolio regularly.

Preparing for future uncertainty involves staying informed, reviewing your financial plan, diversifying income streams, and continuing financial education.

Chapter 15: Building Multiple Streams of Income: Diversifying Your Earnings for Financial Freedom

Relying on a single source of income can be risky, especially in an unpredictable job market or during economic downturns. Building multiple streams of income allows you to diversify your earnings, reduce financial stress, and accelerate your journey toward financial independence. In this chapter, we will explore the importance of having multiple income sources, various ways to generate additional income, and strategies for managing these streams effectively.

15.1 Why You Need Multiple Streams of Income?

In today's fast-paced, ever-changing economy, having multiple streams of income is more important than ever. By diversifying your income sources, you can better withstand financial challenges, create greater wealth, and reduce dependency on a single paycheck.

The Benefits of Multiple Income Streams:

1. **Financial Security:** When you have more than one income stream, you're not solely dependent on your job or business. If one income source dries up (for example, losing a job or business slowdown), you have others to rely on.

2. **Faster Wealth Building:** Multiple income streams allow you to invest more and build wealth at a faster pace. By earning more money, you have greater capacity to save, invest, and take advantage of compounding returns.

3. **Increased Flexibility:** With multiple income streams, you gain more control over your time and financial situation. You can adjust or focus on specific income sources based on personal preferences, life events, or market conditions.

4. **Diverse Opportunities for Growth:** Each income stream can have its own growth potential. Some streams may be passive, like investments, while others may require more active effort. This combination creates a balanced portfolio of earnings.

15.2 Types of Income Streams

There are several ways to diversify your income. Some sources require more time and effort than others, but all contribute to building a more robust financial foundation. Let's explore the different types of income streams:

1. Earned Income (Active Income):

Earned income is the money you make from your job or business. It's the most common source of income for most people, but it's also limited by the hours you work and the salary you earn.

- **Salaries and Wages:** Income from your job or business is the most traditional form of active income. However, it's usually finite and tied to a specific time commitment.

- **Freelancing and Consulting:** If you have specialized skills, freelancing or consulting is an excellent way to earn additional income outside of a regular job. This could include writing, graphic design, programming, marketing, or coaching.

2. Portfolio Income:

Portfolio income refers to money you earn from investments, such as stocks, bonds, mutual funds, or real estate.

- **Dividends:** Stocks that pay dividends can provide you with regular, passive income. Many companies distribute a portion of their profits to shareholders as dividends.

- **Interest from Bonds:** If you invest in bonds, the interest you receive is considered portfolio income. Bonds tend to offer lower returns than stocks, but they are generally more stable.

- **Capital Gains:** If you buy assets (e.g., stocks or real estate) and sell them for a profit, the resulting gain is part of your portfolio income. Long-term capital gains are typically taxed at a lower rate.

3. Passive Income:

Passive income is money you earn without actively working for it. While setting up a passive income stream often requires an upfront investment of time, money, or both, the goal is for it to generate ongoing income with little ongoing effort.

- **Rental Income:** If you invest in real estate, you can earn passive income by renting out property. Rental income can be consistent, but it requires management (or hiring a property manager).

- **Royalties and Licensing:** If you author a book, create music, or develop intellectual property, you can earn royalties or licensing fees. These payments continue over time, often with minimal effort after the initial creation.

- **Online Businesses:** Online businesses, such as affiliate marketing, drop shipping, or selling digital products (like e-books or courses), can be highly scalable and require little active maintenance once they are set up.

- **Peer-to-Peer Lending:** By lending money to individuals or businesses through peer-to-peer lending platforms, you can earn interest on your investment. This is a relatively passive form of income.

4. Business Income:

Running your own business can generate significant income, but it often requires time, effort, and capital upfront. Business income can be both active and passive, depending on how the business is structured.

- **Traditional Small Business:** This could include any business that requires active involvement, such as a restaurant, retail shop, or service-based business. Your income depends on the success of the business and your involvement.

- **Automated Online Business:** For those looking for more passive income, online businesses that operate without much day-to-day involvement can be an excellent choice. Examples include drop shipping, e-commerce stores, and membership-based websites.

15.3 How to Build Multiple Streams of Income?

Building multiple streams of income isn't something that happens overnight, but it is a strategy that pays off over time. Here's how you can start building your own income portfolio:

1. Assess Your Skills and Interests:

Start by evaluating your current skills, expertise, and interests. This will help you decide which income streams align with your strengths and preferences.

- **Freelancing and Consulting:** If you have a specialized skill, consider offering your services on platforms like Upwork, and Fiverr, or by starting your own consulting business.

- **Online Content Creation:** If you enjoy writing, creating videos, or blogging, you can monetize these through ads, affiliate marketing, or selling digital products.

2. Invest in Assets That Generate Income:

- **Real Estate:** Real estate is one of the best ways to generate passive income. Buying rental properties or investing in real estate investment trusts (REITs) can provide you with consistent income.

- **Stocks and Dividends:** If you're able to invest in stocks, focus on dividend-paying stocks that provide regular income streams.

- **Bonds and Peer-to-Peer Lending:** Bonds offer relatively stable returns, while peer-to-peer lending platforms allow you to lend money to individuals or businesses and receive interest payments in return.

3. Start a Side Business or Online Venture:

- **E-commerce or Drop shipping:** Starting an e-commerce store using platforms like Shopify or Amazon can generate additional income. Drop shipping allows you to sell products without maintaining inventory.

- **Digital Products and Courses:** If you have expertise in a certain area, you can create online courses, e-books, or other digital products to sell. Websites like Teachable or Udemy allow you to monetize your knowledge.

4. Automate and Outsource:

Once your income streams start generating cash flow, automate and outsource as much as possible to maximize efficiency and reduce the amount of time you need to dedicate to each stream.

- **Automation Tools:** Use tools to automate online businesses, social media management, email marketing, and more. Platforms like Zapier and Hootsuite can help streamline your processes.

- **Outsourcing:** Hire freelancers or virtual assistants to handle tasks that are time-consuming or outside your area of expertise. This allows you to focus on growing your income streams.

5. Reinvest Your Earnings:

As you begin to earn from multiple sources, reinvest your earnings back into your income streams. Whether it's investing more in the stock market, real estate, or expanding your business, reinvestment accelerates wealth creation.

15.4 Strategies for Managing Multiple Streams of Income

Managing multiple income streams can be challenging, but with the right strategies, you can make the process smoother and more efficient.

1. Time Management:

Balancing multiple income sources requires effective time management. Create a schedule that allows you to dedicate time to each stream without feeling overwhelmed. Use tools like calendars, task managers, and project management apps to stay organized.

2. Track Your Income and Expenses:

Maintain a financial tracking system to monitor all income and expenses. Use software like QuickBooks, Mint, or Excel to track your cash flow and ensure you are meeting financial goals.

3. Keep Taxes in Mind:

With multiple income streams, you will likely face a more complicated tax situation. Keep accurate records and work with a tax professional to minimize your tax liability.

- **Separate Accounts:** Open separate accounts for each income stream, making it easier to track and manage finances.

- **Tax Deductions:** If you own a business or freelance, take advantage of tax deductions available to self-employed individuals, such as home office expenses, equipment, and business-related travel.

4. Diversify and Rebalance:

Ensure that your income streams are diversified across different industries and types of income (active, passive, and portfolio income). Periodically review and rebalance your income streams to ensure they are aligned with your goals and risk tolerance.

End of Chapter 15: Key Takeaways

1. **Multiple streams of income** provide financial security, faster wealth accumulation, and more flexibility in your life.

2. **Diversify your income sources** by pursuing earned income, portfolio income, passive income, and business income.

3. **Start small and gradually scale** your income streams based on your skills, interests, and financial goals.

4. **Automate and outsource** to save time and optimize your efforts as your income streams grow.

Track and manage your income effectively with time management tools, financial tracking, and tax strategies.

Chapter 16: Mastering Money Mindset: Developing a Wealth-Building Mentality

Building wealth is not just about understanding finances or following investment strategies. It also involves cultivating the right mindset—the way you think about money, wealth, and financial success. Your mindset shapes your financial habits, decisions, and ultimately, your ability to grow and maintain wealth. This chapter explores the concept of money mindset and offers actionable steps for developing a wealth-building mentality.

16.1 Understanding Money Mindset

Your money mindset is the way you view and approach money. It is formed by your beliefs, attitudes, and experiences regarding money. Your mindset influences how you save, spend, invest, and how you deal with financial challenges. Understanding your current mindset is essential to shifting toward one that supports wealth-building.

Types of Money Mindsets:

1. **Scarcity Mindset:** Individuals with a scarcity mindset believe that money is limited. They may feel that there is never enough to go around and that opportunities are scarce. This belief can lead to fear-based decisions, hoarding money, or avoiding investments altogether.

2. **Abundance Mindset:** On the other hand, an abundance mindset believes that there are endless opportunities and resources available. People with this mindset tend to be open to new possibilities, embrace growth, and take calculated risks. They understand that wealth is created through opportunities and hard work.

3. **Fixed Mindset vs. Growth Mindset:**

    o **Fixed Mindset:** People with a fixed mindset believe their abilities and intelligence are static, including their ability to handle money. They may avoid financial risks and believe they cannot change their financial situation.

- o **Growth Mindset:** Those with a growth mindset believe that their abilities can be developed through dedication and learning. They view challenges as opportunities to grow and are more likely to take steps to improve their financial situation.

How Money Mindset Affects Financial Behaviour?

- **Spending Habits:** People with a scarcity mindset might be frugal to the point of being miserly, while those with an abundance mindset may spend more freely, focusing on investing in opportunities rather than focusing on saving every penny.

- **Investment Behaviour:** A fixed mindset may lead someone to shy away from investments, believing they are not capable of understanding them. On the other hand, a growth mindset might encourage individuals to learn about investments and embrace them as a tool for wealth-building.

- **Money Management:** Those with a scarcity mindset may struggle with budgeting and managing their finances effectively, fearing that any expense will reduce their wealth. A growth mindset, however, tends to encourage a more strategic approach, where money is managed to fund future opportunities rather than limiting current satisfaction.

16.2 The Role of Beliefs in Financial Success

Our beliefs about money are often formed early in life and are shaped by our families, culture, and personal experiences. These beliefs can either help or hinder your financial growth. Understanding and changing these beliefs is a key part of developing a wealth-building mindset.

Common Limiting Beliefs About Money:

1. **"Money is the root of all evil."** This belief can make you feel guilty about earning or accumulating wealth. It can cause people to sabotage their financial success or avoid pursuing opportunities because they associate money with negative emotions or moral implications.

2. **"I'll never be rich."** This belief reflects a sense of hopelessness or resignation regarding wealth. People with this mindset might

not take the necessary actions to improve their financial situation because they don't believe they deserve success.

3. **"I have to work hard for every penny."** While hard work is important, this belief can limit your thinking about money. It may cause you to undervalue the importance of leverage, automation, and investing, which can generate wealth with less physical labour.

4. **"There's not enough to go around."** This belief stems from a scarcity mindset and can make you overly protective of your resources. It may also cause you to miss out on opportunities because you fear taking risks or believe others will "take away" your share.

Shifting Limiting Beliefs:

- **Reframe Negative Thoughts:** Start by identifying negative money beliefs and reframe them into positive, empowering statements. For example, instead of thinking, "Money is the root of all evil," reframe it to, "Money is a tool that allows me to create positive change in my life and in the world."

- **Affirmations and Visualization:** Use affirmations to replace limiting beliefs. For example, "I am worthy of wealth," or "Money flows easily into my life." Visualization exercises, such as imagining your ideal financial situation, can also reinforce a positive mindset.

- **Educate Yourself:** Often, negative beliefs stem from a lack of knowledge. By educating yourself about personal finance, investing, and wealth-building, you can replace fear and uncertainty with confidence and empowerment.

16.3 The Power of Positive Financial Habits

Your financial habits are the practical actions that align with your mindset. Positive financial habits are essential for developing and maintaining wealth. If you want to create long-term financial success, it's crucial to adopt habits that support your goals.

Key Financial Habits to Build:

1. **Consistent Saving and Investing:** Make saving and investing a habit. Set aside a portion of your income regularly, even if it's a small amount at first. The key is consistency. Over time, the habit will become ingrained, and your savings and investments will compound.

2. **Budgeting:** A solid budget helps you control your spending and prioritize savings. Track your income and expenses, identify areas where you can cut back, and ensure that you're living below your means. By tracking your spending, you can align your money with your goals.

3. **Pay Yourself First:** Before paying any bills or spending money on discretionary expenses, pay yourself first by contributing to your savings or investments. This habit ensures that you're prioritizing your financial future.

4. **Avoiding Bad Debt:** While credit cards and loans can be useful in specific situations, accumulating high-interest debt (such as credit card debt) can undermine your wealth-building efforts. Pay off debt as quickly as possible and avoid taking on new debt unless necessary.

5. **Emergency Fund:** Build and maintain an emergency fund to cover unexpected expenses, such as medical bills or car repairs. Having this fund in place gives you peace of mind and helps you avoid dipping into investments or taking on debt.

16.4 Developing a Long-Term Wealth-Building Mindset

Building wealth is a long-term endeavour that requires patience, discipline, and the ability to stay focused on your goals. Cultivating a long-term wealth-building mindset means thinking beyond short-term wants and focusing on your future financial freedom.

Key Principles of a Long-Term Mindset:

1. **Delayed Gratification:** Wealth-building requires sacrifice and patience. Instead of spending money on immediate pleasures, focus on investing in your future. Delayed gratification is essential for success in both saving and investing.

2. **Embrace Risk and Opportunity:** Wealth is often built through taking calculated risks. Whether it's starting a business, investing in the stock market, or purchasing real estate, those who build wealth tend to embrace opportunities that others might shy away from.

3. **Continuous Learning:** Wealth-building is a lifelong journey. As you progress, continue to educate yourself about new investment opportunities, financial strategies, and wealth-building habits. The more knowledge you gain, the better equipped you'll be to make informed decisions.

4. **Surround Yourself with Like-Minded People:** Surrounding yourself with people who share similar goals and values can help you stay motivated and focused on your financial journey. Join online communities, networking groups, or seek out mentors who can support and challenge you.

16.5 Creating Your Own Wealth-Building Plan

A wealth-building plan is a roadmap for achieving your financial goals. With the right mindset, you can turn this plan into a reality by breaking down your larger goals into manageable steps.

Steps to Create Your Wealth-Building Plan:

1. **Define Your Goals:** What do you want to achieve financially in the short-term and long-term? These goals might include saving for retirement, buying a home, paying off debt, or building an investment portfolio. Be specific, measurable, and realistic.

2. **Assess Your Current Situation:** Evaluate your income, expenses, debts, and assets. This will help you understand where you stand financially and what changes you need to make to achieve your goals.

3. **Create a Strategy:** Based on your goals, create a strategy that includes savings, investments, debt reduction, and income generation. Make sure your strategy is realistic and sustainable.

4. **Track Your Progress:** Regularly track your progress to ensure you're staying on course. Adjust your strategy as needed to accommodate changes in your financial situation.

End of Chapter 16: Key Takeaways

1. **Money mindset** plays a critical role in your ability to build and maintain wealth. Shifting from a scarcity to an abundance mindset can open up opportunities for growth and success.

2. **Beliefs about money** can either help or hinder your financial progress. Identifying and changing limiting beliefs is key to adopting a wealth-building mentality.

3. **Positive financial habits**, such as saving, budgeting, and investing, support your ability to build wealth over time.

4. **Long-term wealth-building** requires patience, discipline, and the ability to make informed decisions about money. Embrace risk, opportunity, and continuous learning to stay on track.

Creating a wealth-building plan helps you stay focused on your financial goals and provides a clear path to achieve them.

Chapter 17: The Psychology of Spending: Understanding Consumer Behaviour and Managing Impulse Purchases

Understanding the psychology behind spending and consumer behaviour is crucial for managing your finances effectively. We often make purchases based on emotional triggers, societal influences, or instant gratification, rather than logical financial decision-making. By gaining insight into these psychological factors, you can take control of your spending, avoid impulse purchases, and make more informed financial decisions that align with your long-term goals.

17.1 The Science Behind Spending

Every purchase you make is influenced by a combination of psychological and emotional factors. By understanding the science behind spending, you can identify your triggers and take steps to avoid unnecessary expenses.

1. The Influence of Emotions on Spending:

Many of our purchases are made in response to emotions, whether it's stress, boredom, excitement, or happiness. Emotional spending, also known as "retail therapy," can provide temporary relief but often leads to financial regret and buyer's remorse.

- **Stress and Anxiety:** People often shop to cope with negative emotions such as stress, sadness, or loneliness. Buying something new can provide a temporary sense of control and comfort.

- **Happiness and Reward:** Some individuals associate spending with happiness or rewarding themselves. Celebrating a promotion or personal achievement often leads to spending money on things that feel like "treats."

- **Boredom and Instant Gratification:** Shopping can become a form of entertainment when someone is bored or looking for an immediate sense of pleasure. The fast gratification of a purchase can temporarily relieves feelings of emptiness or dissatisfaction.

2. The Role of Cognitive Biases:

Human decision-making is influenced by cognitive biases—mental shortcuts that allow us to make decisions quickly, but sometimes irrationally. These biases can lead to impulsive purchases or financial decisions that aren't in our best interest.

- **Anchoring Bias:** When shopping, the first price you see often acts as an anchor, influencing your perception of what's reasonable. For example, if you see a $500 coat discounted to $200, the $500 price anchors your perception, making the $200 seem like a great deal, even if it's still outside your budget.

- **Social Proof:** People often buy products because others are buying them. The influence of seeing others purchase certain items can trigger a desire to conform, even if the purchase isn't necessary or financially sound.

- **Scarcity Bias:** The perception of scarcity can lead people to make purchases out of fear of missing out. Phrases like "limited-time offer" or "only a few left" create urgency, causing people to buy things they don't necessarily need.

17.2 The Impact of Marketing and Advertising

The marketing industry is built around understanding consumer psychology. From advertisements to in-store displays, companies use persuasive techniques to influence purchasing behaviour. By understanding these tactics, you can become a more conscious consumer and avoid being manipulated by advertising.

1. The Power of Advertising:

Advertisements are designed to trigger emotional responses and influence our purchasing decisions. They often focus on the benefits or status associated with a product rather than its practical value. For example, an advertisement for a luxury car may emphasize prestige, success, and exclusivity rather than the car's safety features or fuel efficiency.

- **Emotional Appeals:** Advertisements often target emotions like happiness, fear, and nostalgia. By associating a product with positive emotions, brands can create a psychological connection that drives spending.

- **Lifestyle Marketing:** Companies often position their products as part of a desirable lifestyle, whether it's luxury, health, or status. This appeals to consumers' desire to improve their lives or fit in with a certain group.

2. The "FOMO" Effect (Fear of Missing Out):

Marketing campaigns that play on the fear of missing out can be incredibly effective in influencing spending behaviour. Limited time offers, flash sales, and countdowns create a sense of urgency and encourage people to act quickly, sometimes resulting in impulse purchases.

- **Urgency and Scarcity:** Limited quantities or time-sensitive promotions (e.g., "Only 5 left at this price!") create urgency, leading people to buy impulsively to avoid missing out.

- **Exclusivity and Status:** Exclusive offers or VIP discounts can make consumers feel like they are part of a select group, triggering a desire to purchase based on status rather than need.

17.3 Impulse Buying: Causes and Solutions

Impulse buying is the unplanned, spontaneous purchase of goods or services. It often happens when you are not actively considering the long-term financial impact of the purchase. Understanding the root causes of impulse buying can help you develop strategies to prevent it.

1. Emotional Triggers for Impulse Purchases:

- **Mood and Emotions:** As mentioned earlier, emotions such as sadness, boredom, or excitement can trigger impulse buying. Shopping can serve as a coping mechanism or a quick fix for emotional needs, leading to purchases that you might regret later.

- **Environmental Factors:** The environment plays a significant role in triggering impulse purchases. Brightly coloured sales signs, music, and even the layout of stores can encourage people to buy without thinking.

- **Visual and Sensory Appeal:** When a product is visually appealing or you can touch, feel, or smell it, it becomes more enticing. This sensory engagement is one reason people often purchase items in stores that they may not have intended to buy.

2. Strategies to Avoid Impulse Buying:

- **Implement the 24-Hour Rule:** Give yourself 24 hours to think about a purchase before you buy it. This waiting period allows you to assess whether the item is absolutely necessary or just an impulse.

- **Create a Shopping List and Stick to It:** Whether you're shopping in person or online, make a list of the items you need and avoid deviating from it. This will help you focus on the necessities and reduce the likelihood of buying unnecessary items.

- **Avoid Triggers:** Identify the specific emotional or environmental triggers that lead to impulse buying, such as certain stores, advertisements, or websites. By avoiding these triggers, you can reduce the temptation to buy impulsively.

- **Set a Budget for "Fun Spending":** Allocate a certain amount of money for discretionary spending each month. When the budget is used up, resist the urge to buy more, knowing that you've already accounted for fun purchases.

- **Use Cash Instead of Cards:** Using cash instead of credit cards can limit your spending, as it's harder to part with physical money than it is to swipe a card. This can reduce impulse purchases and help you stay within your budget.

17.4 The Role of Social Media in Spending

Social media has become a powerful platform for influencing consumer behaviour. Influencers, advertisements, and even peer pressure from friends and family on platforms like Instagram, Facebook, and TikTok can contribute to impulse purchases and overspending.

1. The Influence of Social Media Influencers:

Social media influencers often promote products or services that are trendy, new, or aligned with a certain lifestyle. Their endorsement can create a desire to "keep up" with the influencer's lifestyle, leading to spending decisions driven by social validation rather than necessity.

- **Peer Comparison and Envy:** Seeing friends or influencers display new products or experiences can lead to feelings of inadequacy or the desire to keep up. This phenomenon is often referred to as "social comparison" and can drive impulsive spending decisions.

2. Managing Social Media Spending Triggers:

- **Limit Social Media Exposure:** Limit the amount of time you spend on social media or unfollow accounts that regularly promote products you don't need. This can help reduce the impulse to purchase items just because they are being advertised.

- **Engage with Financially Savvy Content:** Follow accounts that promote positive financial habits, budgeting tips, and saving strategies. This can help shift your focus from consumerism to wealth-building and financial responsibility.

17.5 Creating a Conscious Spending Plan

One of the most effective ways to control your spending and reduce impulse purchases is to create a conscious spending plan. A conscious spending plan is about being intentional with your money and spending in a way that aligns with your financial goals.

1. Evaluate Your Values and Priorities:

Start by evaluating what is most important to you. What are your long-term financial goals? Do you want to pay off debt, build an emergency fund, save for a down payment on a house, or invest for retirement? By understanding your values, you can align your spending with these priorities.

2. Budget for Wants and Needs:

Differentiate between your wants and your needs. Needs are essential for your well-being (e.g., housing, food, utilities), while wants are non-essential items that provide pleasure or convenience (e.g., a new outfit, dining out, entertainment). Ensure that you allocate money for both wants and needs but prioritize your needs before your wants.

3. Limit Lifestyle Inflation:

As your income increases, it's easy to fall into the trap of lifestyle inflation—spending more on non-essential items just because you can afford them. Instead, focus on saving and investing your increased income to grow your wealth rather than increasing your spending on luxury items.

4. Reflect on Your Purchases:

After making a purchase, take a moment to reflect on whether it was absolutely necessary and whether it aligns with your financial goals. This practice of self-reflection helps you identify areas where you can cut back and avoid overspending.

End of Chapter 17: Key Takeaways

1. **Emotions and cognitive biases** play a significant role in spending behaviour. Understanding these psychological factors can help you make more informed financial decisions.

2. **Marketing and advertising** tactics are designed to trigger emotional responses and influence purchasing decisions. Being aware of these techniques can help you resist the temptation to buy impulsively.

3. **Impulse buying** is driven by emotional triggers and environmental cues. Implement strategies like the 24-hour rule and sticking to a shopping list to reduce impulse purchases.

4. **Social media** influences consumer behaviour by fostering peer comparisons and promoting products through influencers. Limit your exposure to these triggers to maintain control over your spending.

Conscious spending involves aligning your purchases with your values and long-term goals. A well-defined spending plan can help you prioritize needs, avoid lifestyle inflation, and reflect on your financial decisions.

Chapter 18: Teaching Financial Literacy to the Next Generation

Passing down knowledge of personal finance is one of the most impactful ways to empower the next generation. Teaching children and young adults the skills to manage money wisely equips them to make sound financial decisions, avoid debt, and achieve financial independence. This chapter focuses on how to introduce financial literacy concepts to young people in an engaging and practical way.

18.1 Why Financial Education Matters?

Financial literacy is a critical life skill that is often overlooked in traditional education. Without this knowledge, young people can fall into common traps such as overspending, accumulating debt, or failing to save for the future.

1. Early Habits Have Long-Term Effects:

The financial habits formed in childhood and adolescence can influence behaviour throughout life. Teaching positive habits early helps young people build a strong foundation for managing money.

- **Good Habits:** Saving a portion of their allowance, budgeting for purchases, and distinguishing between wants and needs.

- **Avoiding Pitfalls:** Teaching kids to resist impulse purchases and to understand the dangers of relying on credit for everyday expenses.

2. The Real-World Impact of Financial Literacy:

Understanding basic financial concepts—such as interest rates, compound growth, and debt repayment—can significantly improve outcomes. Financially literate individuals are more likely to avoid high-interest loans, save effectively, and invest wisely.

18.2 Teaching Money Management to Kids

Introducing money management to children doesn't have to be complicated. By incorporating financial lessons into everyday activities, parents and educators can make learning about money fun and practical.

1. Start with the Basics:

- **What is Money?** Explain the concept of money as a medium of exchange for goods and services. Use physical cash to illustrate denominations and basic math.

- **Wants vs. Needs:** Teach children to distinguish between essential needs (food, clothing, housing) and discretionary wants (toys, treats, games).

2. Allowances and Earnings:

- **Give an Allowance:** Allowances provide a hands-on opportunity for kids to practice managing money. Set a small weekly amount and encourage them to budget it.

- **Chores for Pay:** Link allowances to completing age-appropriate chores to help kids understand the value of earning money through work.

3. Introduce Saving and Goal Setting:

- **The Value of Saving:** Teach children to save a portion of their allowance for future purchases. Use a clear jar or a piggy bank so they can see their money grow.

- **Set Financial Goals:** Encourage kids to set short-term goals (e.g., saving for a toy) and long-term goals (e.g., saving for a bike). This teaches patience and delayed gratification.

4. Learning Through Play:

Games and simulations can make financial education more engaging.

- **Board Games:** Games like *Monopoly* or *The Game of Life* teach concepts like budgeting, earning income, and investing in assets.

- **Pretend Play:** Set up a pretend store where children can "buy" and "sell" items using play money, teaching them about transactions and budgeting.

18.3 Financial Education for Teenagers

Teenagers are at a critical stage for developing financial independence. As they begin to earn their own money or prepare for adulthood, they need guidance on more advanced financial concepts.

1. Earning and Budgeting:

- **Part-Time Jobs:** Encourage teens to take on part-time work to earn their own income. This helps them understand the effort required to make money.

- **Create a Simple Budget:** Teach them to allocate their income into categories such as savings, spending, and giving.

2. The Power of Saving and Compound Interest:

- **Introduce a Savings Account:** Help teens open a bank account to manage their money and earn interest. Explain how compound interest works and the benefits of starting early.

- **Savings Challenges:** Encourage teens to save a specific percentage of their earnings for a set period to reach a goal, such as buying a gadget or funding a trip.

3. Responsible Spending and Credit Awareness:

- **Avoid Impulse Spending:** Discuss the risks of emotional purchases and encourage them to wait 24 hours before making non-essential purchases.

- **Understanding Credit Cards:** Explain how credit cards work, including interest rates, minimum payments, and the risks of carrying a balance.

4. Preparing for Future Costs:

- **College and Student Loans:** Discuss the costs of higher education, scholarships, and the implications of student loans. Encourage them to research affordable options and consider part-time jobs during college.

- **Building a Resume:** Emphasize the importance of internships, volunteering, and extracurricular activities to prepare for career opportunities.

18.4 Financial Guidance for Young Adults

Young adults face major financial decisions, such as managing living expenses, paying off student loans, and starting their careers. This stage is crucial for establishing good financial habits.

1. Creating a Realistic Budget:

- **Track Income and Expenses:** Help young adults create a budget that accounts for fixed expenses (rent, utilities) and discretionary spending (entertainment, dining out).

- **Emergency Fund:** Stress the importance of saving 3–6 months' worth of expenses for unexpected situations.

2. Building and Managing Credit:

- **Start with a Credit Card:** Encourage the responsible use of a credit card to build a credit history. Emphasize the importance of paying off the full balance each month.

- **Check Credit Scores:** Teach them to monitor their credit reports and understand the factors that impact credit scores.

3. Investing Basics:

- **The Value of Time:** Explain how starting early allows them to take advantage of compound growth in investments.

- **Retirement Savings:** Encourage participation in employer-sponsored retirement plans (e.g., 401(k)) or opening an IRA.

4. Avoiding Lifestyle Inflation:

- **Live Within Your Means:** Help them resist the urge to spend more as their income increases. Focus on saving and investing to build wealth.

18.5 Tools and Resources for Financial Education

There are many resources available to teach financial literacy at any age. Parents, educators, and young people themselves can benefit from these tools.

1. Books and Guides:

- **For Kids:** Books like *Money Ninja* or *The Berenstain Bears' Trouble with Money* introduce financial concepts in an engaging way.

- **For Teens and Young Adults:** Books like *The Teen's Guide to Personal Finance* or *I Will Teach You to Be Rich* provide practical advice for managing money.

2. Apps and Digital Tools:

- **PiggyBot (for Kids):** Helps kids track their allowance and set savings goals.

- **Mint (for Teens/Young Adults):** Tracks spending, creates budgets, and offers financial insights.

- **Acorns (for Young Adults):** Encourages investing by rounding up purchases and investing the spare change.

3. Online Resources and Classes:

- Websites like *Practical Money Skills* or *Investopedia* offer free educational materials.

- Platforms like *Khan Academy* and *Coursera* provide financial literacy courses for all age groups.

18.6 Involving Schools and Communities

While parents play a significant role in teaching financial literacy, schools and communities can provide additional support through structured programs and activities.

1. Financial Education in Schools:

- Advocate for personal finance classes as part of the curriculum. Topics could include budgeting, saving, credit, and investing.

- Partner with financial institutions to bring guest speakers or workshops into classrooms.

2. Community Initiatives:

- Libraries, community centres, and nonprofits often host free financial literacy workshops.

- Encourage participation in programs like Junior Achievement, which teaches students about entrepreneurship and money management.

End of Chapter 18: Key Takeaways

1. **Financial literacy** is a lifelong skill that starts with teaching children the basics of money management and evolves into guiding young adults through complex financial decisions.

2. **Age-appropriate lessons** ensure that financial concepts are introduced in a way that resonates with each developmental stage.

3. **Hands-on experiences**, such as earning an allowance or opening a savings account, provide practical applications of financial principles.

4. **Resources and tools**, such as books, apps, and workshops, can make learning about money engaging and accessible.

Schools and communities play a vital role in supplementing financial education, ensuring that all young people have access to this essential knowledge.

Chapter 19: Financial Independence and Retire Early (FIRE) Movement

The Financial Independence, Retire Early (FIRE) movement has gained significant popularity in recent years, inspiring individuals to prioritize aggressive saving and investing to achieve financial freedom early in life. This chapter explores the principles, strategies, and challenges of the FIRE movement, providing a roadmap for those who want to achieve early retirement or financial independence.

19.1 What is the FIRE Movement?

The FIRE movement is a lifestyle and financial strategy that aims to help individuals achieve financial independence at a much earlier age than traditional retirement timelines. By saving and investing a significant portion of their income, participants aim to accumulate enough wealth to live off their investments, freeing them from the need to work.

Core Principles of FIRE:

1. **Frugality:** Prioritize saving overspending by living below your means.

2. **Aggressive Saving:** Aim to save 50% or more of your income, compared to the traditional 15–20% savings rate.

3. **Investing Wisely:** Use compound interest and investment growth to accelerate wealth accumulation.

4. **Freedom from Work:** Achieve financial independence where work becomes optional, not necessary.

19.2 Types of FIRE

There are several variations of the FIRE movement, allowing individuals to choose an approach that aligns with their goals and lifestyle.

1. Lean FIRE

Lean FIRE focuses on achieving financial independence with minimal living expenses. This approach requires strict frugality and a minimalist lifestyle.

- **Target Audience:** People who are comfortable living on a low budget and reducing discretionary expenses.

- **Example:** Living on $25,000 annually by maintaining low housing, transportation, and food costs.

2. Fat FIRE

Fat FIRE is for individuals who desire financial independence while maintaining a higher standard of living. It requires a larger savings goal to support a more comfortable lifestyle.

- **Target Audience:** Those who want to retire early but do not wish to sacrifice luxuries.

- **Example:** Living on $75,000–$100,000 annually, supported by a substantial investment portfolio.

3. Barista FIRE

Barista FIRE is a hybrid approach where individuals achieve partial financial independence and supplement their income with part-time work or side hustles.

- **Target Audience:** People who want a balance between financial freedom and some level of work engagement.

- **Example:** Covering 60% of living expenses through investments and 40% through a part-time job.

4. Coast FIRE

Coast FIRE involves saving aggressively in the early stages of life and then reducing contributions once the investment portfolio can grow passively to cover retirement.

- **Target Audience:** Individuals who want to save aggressively early and reduce work-related stress later.

- **Example:** Saving enough by age 30 to let investments grow untouched until traditional retirement age.

19.3 Steps to Achieve FIRE

Achieving FIRE requires disciplined planning and execution. Below are the key steps to reach financial independence and early retirement.

1. Define Your FIRE Goal

Determine the amount of money you need to achieve financial independence.

- **4% Rule:** Use the rule of thumb that suggests you can withdraw 4% of your investment portfolio annually in retirement without depleting your funds.

    - Example: If you want to live on $40,000 annually, your target portfolio should be $1,000,000 ($40,000 ÷ 0.04).

- Adjust the goal based on your desired lifestyle (Lean vs. Fat FIRE).

2. Optimize Your Budget

Identify areas to cut expenses and increase your savings rate.

- **Track Expenses:** Use budgeting tools like Mint, YNAB, or spreadsheets to monitor spending.

- **Reduce Big Expenses:** Focus on cutting costs in housing, transportation, and food, as these are typically the largest expenses.

- **Eliminate Debt:** Pay off high-interest debts to reduce financial burdens and free up income for saving.

3. Maximize Income

Boosting your income can significantly accelerate your path to FIRE.

- **Advance Your Career:** Seek promotions, negotiate raises, or switch to higher-paying jobs.

- **Side Hustles:** Start freelancing, consulting, or other part-time ventures to generate additional income.

- **Passive Income:** Invest in rental properties, dividend stocks, or other assets that generate regular income.

4. Invest Aggressively

Investing is a cornerstone of the FIRE movement, as it allows your money to grow exponentially over time.

- **Stock Market:** Invest in low-cost index funds or ETFs for diversified growth.

- **Real Estate:** Purchase rental properties to generate passive income and appreciate capital.

- **Tax-Advantaged Accounts:** Maximize contributions to 401(k)s, IRAs, or HSAs to reduce taxes and grow wealth faster.

5. Monitor Progress

Regularly evaluate your financial plan and adjust as needed.

- **Net Worth Tracking:** Use tools like Personal Capital to monitor your portfolio's growth.

- **Annual Reviews:** Assess your savings rate, investment performance, and spending patterns.

19.4 Challenges of FIRE

While the FIRE movement is appealing, it comes with its own set of challenges.

1. Sacrifices in Lifestyle

- Living frugally can feel restrictive and may require giving up luxuries or conveniences.

- Social pressures or the fear of missing out (FOMO) can make it difficult to stay disciplined.

2. Market Volatility

- Investments are subject to market fluctuations, which can impact your portfolio's value.

- Mitigation Strategy: Diversify investments and maintain an emergency fund to weather downturns.

3. Longevity Risk

- Retiring early means planning for a longer retirement period, potentially 40–50 years.

- Mitigation Strategy: Factor in inflation and plan for healthcare costs as you age.

4. Burnout from Aggressive Saving

- Saving a significant portion of income can lead to burnout or feelings of deprivation.

- Mitigation Strategy: Allow room for occasional splurges or hobbies that bring joy.

19.5 Is FIRE Right for You?

FIRE isn't for everyone, and it's important to evaluate whether this lifestyle aligns with your values and goals.

- **Self-Assessment:** Are you willing to prioritize long-term goals over short-term gratification?

- **Flexibility:** Can you adapt your strategy if life circumstances change?

- **Risk Tolerance:** Are you comfortable with the uncertainties of relying on investments?

19.6 Benefits of FIRE Beyond Retirement

The FIRE movement isn't just about retiring early; it's also about gaining financial freedom and flexibility.

- **Career Choices:** Work on your terms, pursue passion projects, or transition to a less stressful job.

- **Time Freedom:** Spend more time with family, travel, or engage in hobbies.

- **Peace of Mind:** Reduce financial stress and live without the fear of paycheck-to-paycheck living.

End of Chapter 19: Key Takeaways

1. **The FIRE movement** empowers individuals to achieve financial independence through disciplined saving, investing, and intentional living.

2. **Variations of FIRE** (Lean, Fat, Barista, Coast) allow for customization based on personal goals and lifestyles.

3. **Critical strategies** include defining a clear goal, optimizing your budget, maximizing income, and investing aggressively.

4. **Challenges** such as market volatility, longevity risk, and lifestyle sacrifices require careful planning and flexibility.

The ultimate benefit of FIRE is the freedom to design your life on your own terms.

Chapter 20: Frugality Tips for Financial Success

Frugality is a cornerstone of financial independence and a core principle of the FIRE movement. Practicing frugality doesn't mean living a life of deprivation—it means intentionally prioritizing spending on what truly matters while cutting unnecessary expenses. Below, you'll find an in-depth exploration of frugality strategies across various aspects of life.

20.1. The Mindset of Frugality

Before diving into specific tips, it's crucial to understand the mindset that drives frugality. Frugality is about maximizing the value of your money by making conscious, intentional decisions. It's not about being cheap; it's about being resourceful.

Key Principles:

1. **Value-Based Spending:** Spend on what brings long-term value or joy and eliminate spending on fleeting desires.

2. **Needs vs. Wants:** Differentiate between essential needs (housing, food) and discretionary wants (designer clothes, luxury items).

3. **Contentment:** Find satisfaction in simple pleasures, reducing the desire for expensive alternatives.

20.2. Frugality in Everyday Expenses

1. Food and Groceries

Food is one of the largest recurring expenses for most households, but it's also an area where savings can add up quickly.

Strategies:

- **Meal Planning:** Plan your meals for the week and stick to a shopping list to avoid impulse purchases.

- **Buy in Bulk:** Purchase non-perishable items like rice, beans, and canned goods in bulk for lower per-unit costs.

- **Cook at Home:** Limit dining out and prepare meals at home. Use leftovers creatively to reduce waste.

- **Shop Generic:** Opt for store-brand products, which often cost significantly less than name brands without compromising quality.

- **Use Cashback Apps:** Leverage apps like Ibotta or Rakuten to earn rewards on grocery purchases.

2. Housing

Housing typically consumes the largest portion of a budget, making it a prime area for savings.

Strategies:

- **Downsize:** Consider living in a smaller home or apartment that meets your needs but costs less.

- **House Hacking:** Rent out spare rooms, host on platforms like Airbnb, or purchase a multi-unit property and live in one unit while renting out the others.

- **Negotiate Rent:** If renting, ask for discounts, especially if you're a long-term tenant or willing to pay upfront.

- **DIY Maintenance:** Learn basic home repair skills to avoid hiring professionals for minor fixes.

3. Transportation

Transportation costs, including car payments, fuel, and maintenance, can add up quickly.

Strategies:

- **Use Public Transit:** Public transportation is often significantly cheaper than owning and maintaining a car.

- **Carpool:** Share rides with coworkers or friends to save on fuel costs.

- **Buy Used Vehicles:** Purchase a reliable used car instead of a brand-new one to avoid rapid depreciation.

- **Walk or Bike:** For short distances, walking or biking can save money while improving health.

- **Maintain Your Vehicle:** Regular maintenance can prevent costly repairs in the long run.

4. Utilities

Reducing utility bills is a simple and effective way to cut costs.

Strategies:

- **Energy Efficiency:** Invest in energy-efficient appliances, use LED bulbs, and insulate your home to lower heating and cooling costs.

- **Smart Thermostats:** Use programmable thermostats to optimize heating and cooling schedules.

- **Unplug Devices:** Unplug electronics when not in use to reduce phantom energy consumption.

- **Conserve Water:** Fix leaks promptly, use water-saving showerheads, and only run dishwashers or washing machines with full loads.

5. Entertainment

Entertainment expenses can often be reduced without sacrificing enjoyment.

Strategies:

- **Streaming Services:** Use one or two streaming services instead of a costly cable package. Share subscriptions with family or friends.

- **Free Events:** Take advantage of free local events, libraries, and parks for entertainment.

- **DIY Hobbies:** Pursue low-cost hobbies like reading, hiking, gardening, or crafting.

- **Limit Subscriptions:** Cancel unused memberships or subscriptions that don't provide sufficient value.

20.3. Frugality in Long-Term Goals

1. Debt Reduction

Reducing and eliminating debt is a critical component of frugality.

Strategies:

- **Debt Avalanche Method:** Pay off high-interest debts first to save the most money on interest.

- **Debt Snowball Method:** Pay off smaller debts first to build momentum and motivation.

- **Negotiate Terms:** Contact lenders to negotiate lower interest rates or payment plans.

2. Savings and Investments

Frugality can help accelerate savings and investment growth.

Strategies:

- **Automate Savings:** Set up automatic transfers to savings or investment accounts to ensure consistent contributions.

- **Maximize Employer Benefits:** Take full advantage of employer-provided retirement plans, especially if they offer matching contributions.

- **Focus on Low-Cost Investing:** Choose low-fee index funds or ETFs to reduce costs and maximize returns.

3. Education and Learning

Lifelong learning can be achieved on a budget.

Strategies:

- **Free Online Courses:** Platforms like Coursera, Khan Academy, and edX offer free or low-cost courses on various topics.

- **Library Resources:** Borrow books, audiobooks, and DVDs from your local library instead of purchasing them.

- **DIY Skills:** Learn practical skills, such as cooking, sewing, or minor home repairs, through free tutorials on YouTube.

20.4. Frugality Hacks for Major Life Events

1. **Weddings**

Weddings are notoriously expensive, but frugality can make them more affordable.

Strategies:

- **Small Guest List:** Limit the guest list to close family and friends to reduce venue and catering costs.

- **DIY Decorations:** Create your own decorations and centre pieces using affordable materials.

- **Off-Peak Scheduling:** Choose a weekday or off-season date for discounts on venues and vendors.

2. **Travel**

Travel doesn't have to break the bank when approached with a frugal mindset.

Strategies:

- **Travel Off-Season:** Book trips during non-peak seasons for lower prices on flights and accommodations.

- **Use Points and Miles:** Earn and redeem credit card rewards for free or discounted travel.

- **Budget Accommodations:** Opt for hostels, Airbnb, or vacation rentals instead of expensive hotels.

3. **Raising Children**

Raising children on a budget requires careful planning and prioritization.

Strategies:

- **Buy Second-Hand:** Purchase used clothing, toys, and baby gear from thrift stores or online marketplaces.

- **Cloth Diapers:** Use reusable cloth diapers instead of disposables to save money over time.

- **Free Activities:** Participate in free or low-cost activities like library story time, community events, or nature walks.

20.5. Mindful Frugality

Frugality is most effective when paired with mindfulness. It's not just about spending less—it's about spending intentionally and aligning financial decisions with your values.

Tips for Mindful Frugality:

1. **Practice Gratitude:** Appreciate what you have instead of constantly striving for more.

2. **Avoid Impulse Purchases:** Implement a 24-hour rule before making non-essential purchases.

3. **Reflect on Priorities:** Regularly assess whether your spending aligns with your life goals.

20.6. Frugality Success Stories

Reading about others who have successfully embraced frugality can inspire and motivate you on your journey. Look for blogs, podcasts, or forums like Mr. Money Mustache, The Frugalwoods, or Reddit's r/Frugal.

End of Chapter 20: Key Takeaways

By practising frugality, you can free up resources to save, invest, and achieve your financial goals faster. It's a skill that grows with time and practice, allowing you to live a richer, more intentional life.

Epilogue

As we come to the end of this book, it is not just the conclusion of these pages but the beginning of a new chapter in your journey. Every idea, strategy, and insight shared here was written with one purpose in mind: to equip you with the tools and confidence to take control of your life and forge a path toward the future you envision.

The steps you take from here may not always be easy, but they will be meaningful. Growth requires courage, persistence, and a willingness to adapt. Along the way, remember that every small effort counts and every decision you make brings you closer to your goals.

This book is not the end of our connection but a stepping stone for your continued exploration. The journey to success and fulfilment is ongoing, and the knowledge you've gained here is just the beginning.

I encourage you to revisit these pages whenever you need guidance, inspiration, or a reminder of your potential. Use the lessons here as a foundation, but don't be afraid to innovate and make them your own. Your story is unique, and so too will be your path to success.

Thank you for allowing me to be a part of your journey. It is my hope that this book serves as a source of strength and direction for years to come. May your efforts lead to accomplishments you're proud of and a life that brings you joy and purpose.

Here's to your continued growth and success!

With heartfelt wishes,
Jayanthi R

9 798889 673926 5